ENDORSEMENTS

Permission Is Granted... will provoke new thoughts that will challenge you to change. If you are satisfied with the present condition of the Church, then this book will offend you. But if you are craving for fresh expressions of your personal and corporate faith that are relevant for today and tomorrow's world, then the words in this book will stir you to action. *Permission Is Granted...*, written by Gary Goodell and Graham Cooke, is strategically thought out, biblically grounded, and filled with vision and faith. Take the dare and let your heart run wild; dream a big dream of a Third-Day Church that has both new wineskins and new wine.

—James W. Goll
Cofounder of Encounters Network
Author of *The Seer*, *Dream Language*, and
The Lost Art of Practicing His Presence

Gary Goodell has been "around the block" concerning the religious world. He has operated in traditional churches and seen all manner of flakiness as people seek to come into their spirituality. Consequently, he has a great perspective over what the Third-Day Church should really look like. *Permission Is Granted...* encourages us that God is bringing great change to what we have known as "church life." You will enjoy reading this.

—Chuck D. Pierce
Glory of Zion International Ministries
Denton, Texas

As the Body of Christ forges ahead in this third millennium, there is a great need for pioneers, fathers, and those willing to "follow the cloud." Gary Goodell has always been this kind of leader, through his many years in his Pentecostal roots of Foursquare, during the renewal days of Vineyard, and now as the apostolic leader of Third-Day churches. His new book, *Permission Is Granted...*, is more than a model; it is a mirror of a lifestyle that Gary and Jane Goodell, as well as those who God has sovereignly connected to them from around the world, have lived and walked for many years. Thank God for those who are willing to write the story, rather than always reading someone else's. I strongly recommend this prophetic manual to all those whom God is leading into the Third Day.

—Jill Austin
Master Potter Ministries
Laguna Hills, California

Gary Goodell will help you understand how God's modus operandi changed when Israel crossed the Red Sea and the Jordan River. Now God is operating in a new way in this third millennium. *Permission Is Granted...* will cause you to realize that this reformation is not so much about theology, but methodology—how many of the methods that worked in the past will not work in this dispensation of time. Gary's understanding of the times will stir the hungry heart to discover, to navigate, and to align with God's blueprints and strategies that are unique to them.

—Bruce Friesen
Lion of Judah Ministries
Victoria, British Columbia

Gary is one of the freshest thinkers of our time. He asks penetrating questions, just as Jesus did. He is willing to sacrifice sacred cows and then serve the meat to the hungry Bride of Christ for her nourishment. If you are looking for more, dinner is served. This book is a dangerous document. She's loaded. But it will help you touch the dream many of us carry—authentic Jesus through the Church.

—Kim Unrau
New Life Church
Kelowna, British Columbia

PERMISSION IS GRANTED
TO DO CHURCH DIFFERENTLY
IN THE 21ST CENTURY

PERMISSION IS GRANTED
TO DO CHURCH DIFFERENTLY
IN THE 21ST CENTURY

Graham Cooke and Gary Goodell

Destiny Image® Publishers, Inc.

P.O. Box 310
Shippensburg, PA 17257-0310

"Speaking to the Purposes of God for this Generation
and for the Generations to Come."

For Worldwide Distribution, Printed in the U.S.A.

ISBN 10: 0-7684-2380-5

ISBN 13: 978-0-7684-2380-8

This book and all other Destiny Image, Revival Press, MercyPlace, Fresh Bread, Destiny Image Fiction, and Treasure House books are available at Christian bookstores and distributors worldwide.

For a U.S. bookstore nearest you, call
1-800-722-6774.

For more information on foreign distributors, call
717-532-3040.

Or reach us on the Internet:
www.destinyimage.com

2 3 4 5 6 7 8 9 10 11 / 09 08 07

DEDICATION

To Janie, my wife, my best friend, my confidant, my inspiration, and my fellow traveler for almost 40 years. This renaissance woman is the quintessential Third-Day lady!

—Gary Goodell

Acknowledgments

I am grateful to:

My two kids, Brian and Becky, for their intellect, their passion, their wit, their patience with Pop, and for their gift of my six incredible grandchildren.

The late Bill (LaVern) and Alice Goodell, my parents and first pastors. Even though they have been with the Lord for many years, I still passionately embrace the heritage of their radical faith and that genetic propensity for "risk taking."

My many mentors and coaches (too numerous to count; many are mentioned in this book) who over the years have taught me how to think, not what to think.

To those lifelong friends, fans, and not-so fans, who have faithfully loved and humored me, even when we disagreed. I will be eternally grateful to this adventurous fellowship of "permission givers" who have incarnated the journey of this book.

And finally, such enormous thanks and gratitude to Graham Cooke for giving himself to this project, but even more so, for being my friend.

—Gary Goodell

TABLE OF CONTENTS

PREFACE

L IKE the Indian scouts of old, ear to the ground, we have been hearing the approaching "hoof beats" of a new and different kind of church coming our way. Some think this new church is directly related to our obsession with the cultural postmodern mind-set. Many others make reference to the release of a new apostolic reformation that will totally change the way we "do" church in the future. Others have concluded that this emerging church is at least, in some indirect way, connected to the "new millennium."

For sure, this new church is a gutsy one. It is a risky one. It will be a church that is willing to go where no one has gone before—a "Buzz Lightyear" church that will go "to infinity and beyond."

Christian Schwartz, a German church-growth researcher suggests that we are in the era of a third reformation. The first reformation took place in the 16th century when Martin Luther fought for the rediscovery of salvation by faith, the centrality of grace and of Scripture. It was recognized as a reformation of theology. The second reformation, according to Schwartz, occurred in the 18th century when personal intimacy with God was rediscovered. He calls this a reformation of spirituality. And now what is upon us in this third reformation is a reformation of structure, or how we actually "do" church.[1]

The first reformation brought us a reform in theology, yet failed to affect the major practices of the church. This new reformation, however, will be a complete overhaul and upheaval of how we have done church for the past seventeen hundred years. This reformation promises to be more like a revolution in its passion to alter how the church functions, both in its life and mission.

Many prophetic voices are calling this the "Third-Day Church," and are actually seeing the true potential for a radical new type of emergent Church. It is in the context of this "third day," this "third millennium," that God spoke to me on two separate occasions in the late 1990s and said, "Permission has been granted to do church differently in the third millennium."

Initially, I assumed that this thought, impression, or inner voice was simply part of my devotions that day as I sat journaling on my laptop. But God would say it again, this time in a pastor's conference I was leading; and this time it hit, and hit hard. Like the laser light on those high-tech guns where you see the "red" dot before the trigger is pulled, this time it went in; it went deep, and every leader in the room felt it.

With at least 50 references to the "third day" in Scripture, from Genesis 1:13 to Second Corinthians 15:4, you have to conclude that this is more than just some futile stretch of a man-made theme, some play on words, or the obsession of a chain reference junkie.[2]

- In Exodus 19:11-16, God has the people get ready because on the third day He is going to come down and manifest His presence.

- In Joshua 1:11 and 3:2, God tells the people to get ready to cross over the Jordan on the third day.

- In Ezra 6:15, the temple is completed on the third day, which relates to John 2:19-21, where Jesus says that He will rebuild the temple, referring to His body—first the natural body, then the spiritual body (see 1 Cor. 15:46) that will be raised on the third day.

- In Esther 4:16, Esther calls a fast for three days; then on the third day, she risks her life by appearing and interceding before the king without having been summoned (see Esther 5:1).

- Hosea 6:2 tells us that after two days, He will revive us so that on the third day we may live in His presence.

- In John 2:1, Jesus performs His first miracle by turning water into wine on the third day at the wedding feast in Cana.

And of course, there are several references to the death, burial, and predicted resurrection of Christ on "the third day."

After a simple look at the journey of the people of Israel, you can easily chart the third-day process. Day one is the place of slavery and captivity and is the process of leaving. Day two is the place of testing where everything familiar and secure has been stripped away; it is where we must cleave to God and His promises that are yet to be realized. Day three becomes the entering into, fighting for, and claiming of our destined inheritance in Him.

So whether it is Jonah being released from the "belly of the fish" on the third day, Jesus being released from the "belly of the earth" on the third day, Abraham seeing far off on the third day, Joshua leading the people of Israel across the Jordan to the Promised Land on the third day, Esther putting on her royal robes and going before the king on the third day, or even Jesus performing His first miracle at the wedding in Cana of Galilee on the third day, the sequence seems pretty clear.

DAY ONE, DAY TWO, DAY THREE

Day one is where we are, where we are stuck, needing change, requiring movement, wanting more. Day two is where we enter this process of letting go, moving on, not looking back, moving toward the given and yet unfulfilled promises of God. Then, of course, day three becomes the culmination, the fulfillment, the victory, the resurrection, and the receiving.

Day one is also when you face your frustrations with the status quo and risk stepping off the bank of familiarity into the vast sea of the unknown, moving into day two, toward day three.

Day two is about waiting, hoping, and patiently standing for an answer not yet received. Day two is about death and dying. It is about allowing your vision to die, for until it dies it cannot really live. This is about that "dark night of your soul." It is a test of your willingness to leave the past and move toward the "new day," the "third day," and pay the full price to get there.

Another unique way my daughter described it to me years ago, was, "Dad, I get it! God doesn't close one door without simultaneously opening another door, but it is hell in the hallway." That is the second day—hell in the hallway!

When we speak of the Third-Day Church, we are speaking prophetically as to how we are being offered new and innovative ways of doing church. Some of these ways seem new in the sense of actually being old, yet untried. Others represent fresh, even currently unconsidered ways to do and be the Church. The first day, then, is how we used to do church. The second day is when we let those old ways die. The third day is when we begin to experiment with new ways to meet, new ways to make more room for His presence, and new ways that we see our mission and purpose as a Church, both locally and regionally.

NEW WAYS OF DOING CHURCH

To even consider something new, something different, to even think of leaving the first day—the day of the tried forms, the current habits, or the day of our present traditions—assumes that there has to be some degree of internal and/or external dissatisfaction brewing. This must be true to lure someone towards risking the tried and true and jumping off the safe to the deep waters of "having never been here before."

Merely leaving the dock of security is torment enough to keep us in the first day. The third day is not merely an adjusted or adapted or retrofitted first day; it means an impassioned willingness to leave the familiar, the known, and the seen, going for the unfamiliar, the unknown, and the unseen...and like Abraham of old, not looking back.

It requires a genuine leap of faith, losing sight of the land of self-reliance on your way to a new destination. It is the knowledge that in that notorious middle, during that second day, in that place of transition between the abandoned and the found, that everything gets shaken, everything gets tested, and you die. The Latin word for this place is *limina*. It means threshold. It is that place you step into, not knowing where you are going, but also not looking back. It is that in-between place. In Hebrews 11:8, we read that Abraham stepped off his map as he decided by faith to go where he didn't know.

The thought of the pain, the fog, and the disequilibrium of the second day, keeps so many of us stuck in the first day—stuck, as it were, in doing things the same way week after week, meeting after meeting, not wanting to rock the boat, not wanting to be misunderstood or labeled a misfit or maverick or a loose cannon. Nor do we want to appear as though we don't know what we are doing or where we are going.

So, why not leap? Why not jump? Why not head into that dark day two? To not do so is to eventually become so stale, so brittle that the old wineskin plugs up, corks up, no longer receiving, no longer releasing.

As the scenario goes, you will not get to the third day unless you step out of the first day and are willing to endure the hazard pay of the second day.

This is not some philosophical diatribe. Inside all of us exists, at least to some degree, a divine dissatisfaction that has been percolating or brewing for quite some time, possibly years, maybe even a lifetime.

Yet, deep in our hearts, at our core, in our passions and in our dreams, we have known all along that there is something more, something deeper, something beyond what our comfort zones have allowed us to experience or touch. To not take that risk, to not take that leap of faith, means to die a slow, agonizing death.

TIME FOR EXPERIMENTATION

Most experimentation begins in the head long before it is ever discussed, let alone implemented. It means giving yourself permission to daydream about things like how the worship service could flow a bit differently, how more people could be involved in the actual meeting, or how the structure or infrastructure of the church could be modified for optimum results. It means admitting that you are tired of mimicking some stereotypical way of church life and you want to be a prototype as you risk obeying the God of the Church who is calling you into that fresh metamorphosis of the "third day."

Wherever it starts, it does require action, some form of response. Like the age-old proverb, "Three frogs sat on a log, all three decided to jump...so how many were left?" And, of course, the answer is all three. They decided, but they didn't actually jump.

For years I have been asking my fellow pastors an open-ended question, "If you couldn't fail, would you do church differently?" I don't have to tell you how many of them give me a resounding, "YES!" I have also asked myself the same question many times. And despite my fears, my personal "yes" finally forced me into action, and the experiment began.

THE FELLOWSHIP OF PERMISSION GIVERS

In this little church on the West Coast, we began our third-day journey. We do not perceive ourselves as having arrived, or as some new elitist, end-time group trying to lay claim to some current "now" word for the total Body of Christ.

We remain a simple band of brothers and sisters, a rather unorthodox fraternity of pilgrims. We profoundly and intentionally want to encourage one another in doing church differently, and hopefully more effectively in this postmodern third millennium.

This book is a journal of one church's journey into the "third day," experimenting with new ways of "doing" church. We invite you to think outside your normal grid, color outside the lines, dream outside your restrictive boundaries, and peek into our process as we have treaded the waters of this third-day experiment.

—Gary Goodell

ENDNOTES

1. Wolfgang Simson, *Houses That Change The World* (Waynesboro, GA: Authentic, 2001), 6-7.

2. Ibid.

INTRODUCTION

THE world around us is full of change. Keeping pace with man's inventiveness is amazingly difficult. No sooner does a breakthrough piece of engineering hit the market than it is made smaller, more compact, and more powerful. It seems that whatever you buy is out-of-date before you learn how to use it properly.

International boundaries are changing; different nations are forming or re-forming. Economies everywhere are going through profound change with the realization that no economy will ever be safe again. Some changes affect not only the way we live but also our perception of who we are as human beings.

Despite the immensity of change taking place in our world, very few of us have learned to deal with change in a healthy way. Without being aware of reasons why, we seem to put up instinctive and devious barriers to anything remotely looking like change. There is something in most people that profoundly dislikes transition, which causes them to do amazing things in order to not have to go through any change at all.

Transition is an adventure into the unknown with all the attendant risks that the uncharted can formulate around us. Change provokes our hearts because it challenges the status quo. It makes us feel uneasy and vulnerable because it takes us into territory where we have never been before. We are happy to talk about Abraham going out without knowing where he was going, simply trusting God to get him there (see Heb. 11:8). However, when it is our turn to make the journey of faith, it is a different matter. God has His own road maps for times such as these. The old ones are useless to us, and the new ones are completed as we go!

Every change involves a letting go of one thing to reach out for what is next. It is death by installments—the slow death of our mindsets, our attitudes, perceptions, and paradigms with apparently nothing obvious to take their place. That is, we see only the replacement concept as we journey. We don't just see it, though; we experience it. Sometimes our experience is first, and we go through something that we understand only in retrospect. It is important, therefore, if we are to journey with the Lord into new lands, that we build in time to reflect and review where we are and where we have come from. Our road map to faith must be kept up-to-date and relevant for anyone else coming after us.

Pioneers draw the maps; they seldom enjoy them! Every day's journey into the new is accompanied by a slow and, at times, painful letting go of the old. There is a death process to be worked through in transition. Future fruit comes from present death (see John 12:24).

The Holy Spirit will, if we allow Him, teach us how to be present to the moment with God. There is a God-consciousness that is so compelling that we need never worry again. There is a peace so profound that it is unshakable. There is a rest in God so potent that the enemy fears it. (Rest is a weapon against evil.)

In order to be alive to God in this way, we must surrender to Him and to everything He brings. He allows in His wisdom what He could easily prevent by His power. The dying daily that is Paul's description involves a death-to-self process. Change is the pivotal point of that process. If you enjoy God's life, you cannot fear change. Where He is present, resistance has died.

Death, the understanding of change, liberates us to experience the adventure of new things. We welcome the risk because His life fizzes in our bloodstream. He sparkles with new gifts, new realms, fresh anointing, and different challenges to faith and love.

His great power will pitch us into battle with no other thought but that His great love will shield us from the enemy. He is careful and carefree at the same time. Change is an opportunity to grow more like Him and to continue the sampling of all He has to offer. He Himself never changes; that is part of His beauty. He is so utterly faithful and unchanging that we always know exactly where we are in His heart.

He wants to impart that same unchanging nature to us so that we can partake of this aspect of His divine nature. Though unchanging in Himself, He causes ceaseless change round about Him. To know Him is to be changed by Him. He loves the journey that we are on. He has carefully thought through all the stages that we will experience. Death and life combine in Him. Unchanging changeableness is part of His mystique. Find meaning in Him, and you will understand your journey so much better. Everything begins and ends in Him, the Alpha and Omega of change.

The inevitability of change is made enjoyable by His presence. As we submit to each process, our appreciation of the journey grows and our faith increases. Change comes from within. Everything that God does in us comes from the inside to the outside. That is why our inward development is more important than the outward circumstances. If we give the Lord Jesus the ground He requires on the inside of our life, then each present set of external challenges shall diminish, if not disappear.

We will be excited about change because we are excited about the Lord. Our road map is being drawn as we experience life in Christ. But if we keep hitting the same landmarks in our life, it is probably because we have resisted change from within.

Change helps us grow, and growth is part of life. Without challenge there is nothing to overcome, so faith cannot grow. This lack of expectation creates smallness in mind and heart.

PROCESS IS RELATIONAL

Transition is a process; it is a series of steps and stages that take us from one realm to another. There is a rhythm to life and a cadence to walking with God. Each of us must be in tune with our inner man before the Lord. When Jesus spoke in parable form, He spoke of shepherds, fishermen, and farmers, putting people in touch with the rhythm of their existence and teaching them the movement and the tempo of the spirit life.

In nontechnological times, people lived at a different pace or beat. They were in tune with nature and its ways and processes. Their ability to survive depended on that knowledge. And what is true in the natural is true in the spirit (see 1 Cor. 15:46). Our walk with God is not separate from our employment track or our natural affiliations.

With regard to these days, people live by clock and calendar. We schedule people into diaries depending on actual time, not the rhythm of our life. In other days, people did things after sowing, plowing, or harvesting. The natural seasons were the only calendar they wanted or needed. However, these days we are governed by deadlines, time constraints, and schedules. Few people eat when they are hungry, sleep when they are tired, or get up when they are rested. When we wake up two hours early, most of us stay in bed because it isn't time to get up.

All this is very well, but what is the point? The point is we have lost access to our rhythm—the ability to flow through life from within, to have the form and essence of our life be prescribed by our inner voice.

Our world is too functional, too structured and contrived. There is little rest and peace in the process of how we are forced to live. God ordained that our lives should fit a natural and spiritual process. Society and civilization largely have robbed us of both. Physically we are made up of a procession of movements. Psychologically and spiritually the same creative process applies.

For example, rest is an important process in all three areas. Physical rest in sleep, peace of mind, and the act of trusting and not being anxious are part of our rhythm of life before God. Food intake is good for the body, just as reading or conversation is for the mind, and prayer for our spirit.

The world is full of functional paradigms while we were created to live in relational ones. The loneliness and lack of friendship and companionship we feel is damaging to our health. *"It is not good that man should be alone..."* (Gen. 2:18b).

Relational process is about the journey we make with God and one another. The functions of life now rule us. Everyone wants to know what we do rather than who we are. People define their lives by geography, job title, and performance. In this busy functional paradigm, we seldom have real time for people, whereas we have surface relationships with many people. We wear social masks of politeness that hide our fears, worries, and inner thoughts. We do not reveal our true inner self because we are afraid of rejection. Our fear of rebuff does not allow us to go deep with people around us. We want to be loved, but the process of real love involves the true revelation of self.

Transition is about the journey of relationships as much as anything else—learning to trust, to be open and honest, to understand and be understood, to accept and approve, and in turn find acceptance and approval. Transition is about connecting with one another as we draw the road map of life in the spirit together. It is about connecting through our fears and concerns, dreams and aspirations, joys and delights, dislikes and annoyances. Whenever we hide part of ourselves for fear of discovery, we disconnect or fail to connect with people at that point.

PROCESS INVOLVES CRISIS

Transition usually throws us together in circumstances that are far less than ideal. Transition involves crisis. Yet crisis leads us to process, through which our road map will deliver us to a new place of promise if we faithfully complete this particular leg of the journey. It is hazardous and arduous but exhilarating and inspirational, all at the same time. The difficulty lies in the fact that we don't see transition coming, mainly because we do not live from within.

However, when we live from the inner man of the spirit, we detect nuances, like a sailor detecting subtle shifts in the wind, or a farmer the smell of early rain. These signs of change cause us to reflect and move closer to the person of God through prayer and worship. We begin to ask for grace and wisdom because we feel something is changing. Our early warning system is working. Most churches have an early warning system. They are called prophets, or they could be people with a prophetic/intercessory gifting.

The difficulty is that the prophet speaks about change and transition while the rest of us are in a place of safety and blessing. Hence, churches seldom take such a word and process it internally. The prophecy is given so that we can make subtle changes to our perspective, the way we position ourselves before God, and our petition to Him for us to be faithful in the coming crisis. Many people heed storm warnings too late and put themselves in places of needless risk.

If we lived in a relational paradigm of sensitivity to God and one another, we would go through life evenly and with more calm.

A friend in the ministry, Steve Chua, once told me that the Chinese word for crisis is made up of two concepts involving danger and opportunity.

The danger comes through disruption. Crisis will often involve a storm. We are caught up in a tempest of different circumstances colliding together. It is a time of commotion, assault, agitation, passion, strife, and outburst.

Every spiritual storm has two halves. The first breaks upon us and finds us ignorant and confused. Maybe we didn't heed the early warning system when it sounded the alarm; possibly our internal man was not in position and listening. Then suddenly we are in the midst of crisis and our relationships come under intense pressure.

PROCESS IS PRIMARILY INTERNAL

If people have no internal frame of reference, they lash out, under pressure, externally. Because they are involved in a functional paradigm, they connect on that level. Other people are at fault because this or that did not happen; we relate through function. We get angry and frustrated and look for a way out on a physical, emotional level. We stop to ask why this is happening on a physical level, but our answers at this stage do not give us the wisdom to see beyond the natural. The outer man sees the danger and reacts to it, lashing out indiscriminately, apportioning blame, and living on survival instincts of self-preservation. Our prayers are for deliverance and escape.

The inner man understands the danger but also recognizes the opportunity that God is presenting. Our inner perspective helps us position ourselves in line with God's objective and pray in accordance with His will. Those living from the inner realm see beyond the natural into the realm of the Spirit, so they wait patiently and with praise and honor for the Lord Jesus to reveal Himself.

Transition is about revelation and the process needed to make it real and experiential. We miss the profound truths and the deeper works of God when our paradigm is functional and not relational. If we are unprepared when the storm hits us, we take it on board in our soul, not our spirit. Our soul is the outer man reacting through our body, the outermost part of our being.

We have a conflict of two natures within us—the spirit versus the flesh (see Gal. 5:17). Our soul and our carnal nature (flesh) interact together. Our soul is made up of our mind, emotions, and will. These elements can be drawn inward into the realm of the spirit through the attention and faithfulness of the inner man toward God.

Alternatively, they also can be drawn into an external perspective through relationships, circumstances, and influences. This external perspective with no inward support will be the vehicle through which worry, fear, anger, bitterness, and rejection can take hold of our hearts. We will be agitated, vexing, and difficult to live with.

Revelation is the revealing of who God is and what He is doing. It impacts our lives and changes our viewpoint. It divides spirit from soul, enabling us to live before God and experience what He is releasing to us (see Heb. 4:12).

Though our outward man is crumbling under the assault of life and circumstances, our inward man retains a balance before God, which brings a constant renewal (see 2 Cor. 4:16-18). The inner man does not look at what is seen but goes beyond that to a level of perception that is more powerful and life changing.

In all tribulations and transitions, it is the revelation of God's intention that allows an amazing strengthening to be released into the inner man by the glorious power of the Spirit. There is a change within, which enables faith to rise and understanding to appear, causing us to be filled and to abide in a realm of power that can achieve more for us than we ever thought possible in the circumstances.

Transition is about the discovery and connection of the inner man of the heart toward God (see Eph. 3:13-21). It is about discovering the rest of God (see Heb. 4) and being at peace in Him. It is restoring our relational paradigm with Almighty God. It is about breakthrough into an inner place of the spirit and learning how to remain there. Your inner man is the restful presence of Jesus in the external turmoil of your surroundings (see Mark 4:36-39).

This is the opportunity that God is giving to us in the crisis of transition. He is holding out the very process of inward change and development. In crisis we put our lives firmly into His care and we obey Him implicitly! Crisis, transition, and process open a door on a personal and corporate level for the people of God to come to know Him, experience Him, and be changed by Him. Crisis is the door of inward opportunity opening through the danger of external circumstances.

The Spirit searches all things in our lives and enables us to know the mind of the Lord (revelation) as well as to experience what God wants to give us in the situation (see 1 Cor. 2:10-16).

Many times we are unprepared for the storm that breaks over us. However, if we are used to living from our spirit, we can retreat there to our secret place and wait patiently for God. Yet if we have not fully learned that discipline of grace, we may succumb to worry and fear. Then we will be tossed to and fro by circumstances and unsurrendered thought-processes. The inner man of the spirit is the anchor for the soul.

Here, in our distress, the kindness of God will reveal itself to us. He really wants us to succeed in crisis. He wants us to go through the door of opportunity and not be sidetracked by the difficulty in the situation. He will give us a second opportunity to succeed.

Every storm has two halves divided by peace (the eye of the storm). Churches going through difficulty need apostolic or prophetic presence to give them Heaven's perspective. These gift ministries can enter into a situation to bring peace and provide revelation. They stand with one foot in our past and the other in our future. They can tell us where we have been and where we are going, and they can bring both together into our present to help us make sense of where we are now! They give us the revelatory rationale for what is happening.

Having understanding does not save us from the second half of the storm. However, now, through the input of revelation, we have a compass reading to take us in the direction that God wants us to travel. Therefore, we can endure the change because we know what God wants to achieve. Now we can let go and let God have His way.

On a personal level, we may be going through tough circumstances that we are failing to process internally. We need to look and listen for the sweet voice of reason to come to us. It may come in a sermon, through a book we are reading, by a Scripture we are studying, from a prayer we receive in ministry, in a letter or card, through a prophetic word, or in a telephone call from a concerned friend. The point is, it will come! Many times, we miss it because our soul wants to hear only about deliverance, so we sift every word and discard those not compatible with our soulish desires. The inward man knows that process is the key to all God's dealings with His people. Life is a journey. A friend of mine, Mary Dennison, once told me, "Don't get so hung up on your destination that you forget to enjoy the journey!"

Soulish activity often leads us into realms of protectionism. It puts a hard exterior, a protective cover, over our sensitive areas of mind and heart. Like a bulletproof vest, it protects the wearer from any adverse circumstances. Whereas the spirit man finds his protection in the love of God. He knows that God is our secret place, refuge, fortress, high tower, hiding place, and holy habitation.

When the soul protects itself, it doesn't realize that the hard outer casing also prevents relationships from forming with God and people. The wearing of this casing is irksome. Not only will it give you a form of protection, but it also encases all your irritations. They are locked in with you!

The inner man gets rid of such things by having open communion with God and people, while the outer man is imprisoned by these things until release occurs. Worries, fears, frustrations, and irritations begin to adversely affect our personalities because they have no place of release. We become angry, resentful, bitter, and vengeful in all that inner turmoil. Our health suffers, and we are unhappy, negative, and contemptuous in our personalities.

If we have no way of dealing with these issues, they simply stay with us. They never leave and continue to act on the inside of us. Each unresolved issue becomes another layer that has to be peeled off if we are going to enjoy life. The accumulation of unresolved issues grows into a barrier, a shell that covers our heart and emotions. Frustration is the result of all these unresolved conflicts. We have a short fuse; we get exasperated easily. We feel thwarted by other people. We do not want to allow them to have a viewpoint. We listen only to give our opinion. While they are talking, we are formulating our riposte.

Transition cracks the shell of our personality and breaks open our hardness. Frustration is a key to development. Part of our frustration is caused by a history of disappointments and unresolved issues, creating dissatisfaction and unfulfillment. We half expect to get thwarted again and so we get our shot in first. We have learned how to see the flaws, the cracks, the negatives in situations and people because our protective shell looks to guard itself against intruders.

PROCESS RELEASES POTENTIAL

Through the prophetic side of my ministry, I have had hundreds of contacts with people who were very negative toward me because they were under the illusion that I could see right through them. Actually, I prefer to see the good in people. No one can hide his or her rubbish for too long though; truth will always come out. A prophet looks for the treasure in the earthen vessel and brings it to the surface. We are on a treasure hunt, seeing people with the eyes of the Lord Jesus—the kindest person I have ever known.

God always speaks to our potential. Gideon was alone, frightened, angry, and disillusioned. He had lots of questions and reservations and a tremendously low self-esteem. When God came on his scene, he was hiding away, making bread in a winepress (like you do when you're depressed). There were so many things the Lord could have said. He could have ministered deliverance or rebuked him for his lifestyle and attitude. Instead, the Lord spoke warmly to him: "Hello, Gideon. The Lord is with you, O valiant warrior!" (see Judges 6:12).

God spoke to what was noble in Gideon, and it rose up within him. Whatever we speak to in people, rises up! If we speak to their flesh and find fault, the flesh will rise up and there will be an angry frustration. If, however, we speak to their spirit, to their potential, then the treasure of Christ that is within them will surface. We will find that as the treasure rises, people will automatically deal with any issue in their life that is preventing that treasure from being revealed. In this way, prophecy is an inspiration to enable people to change and an encouragement to see themselves as God sees them. It releases the wonderful presence of the Comforter to enable them to deal with any rubbish in their lives. We simply have to love God and all His ways. The kindness, the grace, and the thoughtfulness of the Lord are outstanding!

However, when people do not know how the Lord thinks or works, they tend to think the worst. So people have blanked me out in various ways in order to not be exposed. They do not understand that God is more interested in exposing their potential than He is in the stuff it is buried in!

Our frustration has to be cracked open. Signs of pain are usually signs of resistance as well. It shows us where we need to be healed. In the natural, a cut or a bump denotes the area needing medical care. Likewise, in the spirit, our pain is a pointer to our healing. Frustration also shows us where the point of breakthrough is going to come in our shell. Frustration is the key to our ongoing resistance. It tells us where the hammer of the Lord will apply itself to the hard shell around us. Your frustrations and pain are clues to your transition. The process will involve God breaking into those areas to bring healing, release, and empowerment. He loves you too much to let you stay in that place!

Watch for the signs; the Comforter will open your eyes and teach you if you ask Him. He is quite brilliant at this aspect of relating to God's people. Enjoy Him!

In the mercy of God and out of our abiding relationship with Him, we are better equipped to perceive transitional moments and seasons. This gives us the power to choose to cooperate ahead of time, which is very significant in our relationship with the Lord. We can become prophetic in our own development, thwarting the plans of the enemy as we grow in our spirit. This can be a pleasant and welcome experience—maintaining our tranquility of mind and heart despite the pressure of life.

Other areas of transition are unseen and also unpredictable. We learn how they are going to turn out only as we walk closely with the Lord. Indeed, that is the point of some changes and upheavals. As well as helping to shape the direction of our heart and life, they also deliver us to a new level of dependency on the Lord Jesus. At first, they make us vulnerable, insecure, and inadequate, which is excellent. Actually, these are three of the entry points into the grace of God where we stand in hope of His glory. That is the reason why Paul was so pleased with weakness, (see 2 Cor. 12:7-10); he knew it was an entry point into God's grace. He became both most glad and well content. He had a revelatory rationale for what was bothering him. He knew the process that God was using (through the difficulties he was encountering) to bring him to a new place in the spirit. Paul's revelation of God's grace was not big enough for the level of warfare he was experiencing; hence, the thorn in the flesh. It was allowed by the Lord to bring Paul into a deeper relationship with Himself. The best way to combat darkness is to receive greater light. Having an increase of revelatory rationale for the events of life is a prerequisite for greater spiritual growth.

—Graham Cooke

Section One

THIRD-DAY DEVELOPMENT

Chapter One

CREATING PARTNERSHIPS
OF MUTUAL WORTH AND VALUE

A LL real partnerships are based on a shared vision that combines personal dreams with corporate identity. If we are to make disciples of all people, we must know certain things about them. We must know them as people...with their strengths and weaknesses. God chooses the foolish, the weak, the base and despised. He loves the unwise, those who are not strong, who seem ignoble...and lacking in honor! (See 1 Cor. 1:26-29.)

It is important to know that we have to develop wholly imperfect people and love the job of improving their character. We need a vital commitment to grace and lovingkindness. Leaders must demonstrate the nature of God! It requires a depth of patience and longsuffering. Transforming people is not easy. Into each man and woman God breathes His love and commitment. He gives them dreams and callings.

And He gave some, apostles; and some, prophets; and some, evangelists; and some, pastors and teachers; for the perfecting of the saints, for the work of the ministry, for the edifying of the body of Christ: till we all come in the unity of the faith, and of the knowledge of the Son of God, unto a perfect man, unto the measure of the stature of the fullness of Christ: that we henceforth be no more children, tossed to and fro, and carried about with every wind of doctrine, by the sleight of men, and cunning craftiness, whereby they lie in wait to deceive; but speaking the truth in love, may grow up into Him in all things, which is the head, even Christ: from whom the whole body fitly joined together and com-pacted by that which every joint supplieth, according to the effectual working in the measure of every part, maketh increase of the body unto the edifying of itself in love (Ephesians 4:11-16 KJV).

All the fivefold gifts are consultants for the Kingdom of God; and they are leaders, trainers, and equippers of people.

PURPOSE OF FIVEFOLD MINISTRIES

Their purpose is wholly centered on development: How do we make the Body of Christ reflect the glorious nature of God? We equip every believer for service and to do work of the ministry. There are no super-stars and no ministry elite in the Body of Christ. We must teach Body-building as a way of life in the Spirit. The Body can grow in power and significance only when every member is leaning on God in sensitivity and power.

Body-building is a vital ministry. Ensuring that every member is specifically trained and equipped to serve the Lord is a crucial part of any leader's role in the church.

In order to take cities and turn them upside down for God, it is essential that we develop the unity of faith to a high level of power, cooperation, and significance. Every believer must know who Jesus is for them personally and be able to bring other people into the same place in Christ that they occupy.

Developing maturity in people at every opportunity is not an option; it is an essential ingredient of church life. They must experi-ence how to discover and depend on God for themselves. Good lead-ers increase everyone's capacity for fullness in Christ. As people grow, they ensure they are constantly filled and able to develop real stature in the Spirit.

We cannot take chances with the maturity of our people. There is no place for childish immaturity, ignorance of truth, or low character. Our people must be trained in the Holy Spirit to live a life where they are not subject to events, not easily deceived, and not taken in by the world, the flesh, or the devil.

It is our pleasure to grow people of love and truth who know how to move in both, to grow them into all aspects of Christ, and to develop a commitment to the whole Body and specifically the part they are joined to in fellowship and ministry.

However, it is impossible to do any of that if we treat people like sheep, collectively. A good shepherd knows every sheep individually; that's why he is able to go after the one who is lost.

Jesus knew His own sheep by name (see John 10:3), and His sheep know His voice (see John 10:4). This metaphor was a figure of speech concerning the personal relationship between the sheep and the Good Shepherd. The leaders in the church are also sheep. Jesus spoke to Peter three times concerning His people—"Look after My sheep, not yours" (see John 21:15-17).

Our goal is to facilitate the development of every believer in Christ. Corporate vision cannot be imposed from the top down. It has to grow from the ground up. It's like a painting. Broad brush strokes may come from leadership, but fine detail is supplied by the people.

While broad brush strokes come from the leadership regarding the vision of the house another brush is required for the fine detail that reveals the intricate nature of the picture being painted. This relates to the fact that all good leaders know how to facilitate people into their own personal vision and then see the release of that to complete the corporate picture and anointing.

Everyone has a dream. Good leaders have the Father's touch to expedite the dreams of God through the hearts of His people. Vision must grow from the ground up in order to fully release the anointing of the corporate man.

It's important to discover what the Lord has put into the hearts of His people—where their God-given dreams can serve the church and develop their potential. That is specifically what we equip people to do—train them to fulfill God's dream over their life.

ACTION PLANS

Actions plans have two elements—general and specific. Everyone in the Body should have an action plan for his or her life and calling.

The general part should cover life and lifestyle. It should be concerned with an identity and character in Christ. It should cover relationship, sensitivity, and life with the Holy Spirit. It will be involved with the process of developing holiness, righteousness, and integrity.

The action plan should place high regard on our relationships both with the Father and with people. It will, therefore, reflect the loving nature of God in both directions—to us and through us.

The action plan will affect our intimacy, worship, and devotional life with the Father because it will enable us to focus on Him and create goals for the process that He has outlined. This will have a huge effect on our capacity to meditate (think deeply about God) as a part of our normal routine of life.

The action plan should also be specific to our calling with a regard to developing our anointing and authority to serve and minister alongside the Holy Spirit. We need to know how to minister to people, how to release them into their freedom and their identity in Christ.

The action plan should help us to determine what kind of training initiatives we need to develop corporately in the Body and enable us to specifically align people in clusters together so that we serve in team and in unity of purpose.

The challenge is to see where individual vision complements and adds to the corporate and to also see where the corporate vision can be adjusted to fit the individual one! We need a framework that breathes, that allows leaders to lead but gives individuals the opportunity to hear God and follow His plan for themselves. It creates opportunity for unique and powerful partnerships to emerge.

This is literally double vision. When our heart is set on partnership, we discover the wonderful joy and paradox of the individual and corporate vision. We serve both as good leaders. On the other hand, poor leadership elevates the corporate above the individual, and so the paradox becomes a parody of the heart and intentionality of God.

Today, people are excluded because they "don't fit in." In addition, people have to subjugate their own dream in order to serve the vision of the house. A box has been created that captures people instead of captivating them. We create rules of behavior to keep people in the confines of what we determine is decent and in order. The problem is that our sense of order comes out of a functional paradigm that is cemented in the need for leaders to possess, acquire, and control. This is eros love—love with a hook, love that uses people but does not fulfill them. The box becomes the coffin of their dreams and aspirations.

God's sense of order is always earthed in relationships; therefore, it constantly adjusts to people as they grow, change, and become more of who they are in Christ. Whereas, order in a functional paradigm never adjusts to people. It remains static and expects people to adapt to it. When the system is more important than the individual, then we become a Pharisee and are guilty of the sin of expedience; the individual should suffer for the whole (see John 11:50).

A society that values the individual will always rise to the highest place of its power because this value enshrines integrity, decency, and honor. But when we cease to honor the weakest member, we are diminished as a company of called-out people.

Know this—the sin of expediency among leadership is causing tens of thousands of people to leave the church in order to pursue a relationship with God that enables their dream to both flourish and be fulfilled. People are searching for such meaning-seeking environments that will develop them to be the best they can be for God.

New, permission-giving churches are emerging all over the landscape of the Kingdom. Control from leadership is diminishing in favor of the fruit of self-control that arises out of people being trained to be responsible and mature in the Spirit.

Vision changes as we grow up in Christ. Vision requires redefinition as we achieve goals set by the Holy Spirit. Every vision can last for only three to five years before major redefinition is needed, simply because people grow, change, and become more Christlike. Therefore, we must reinvent our relationships in the same time period lest our real friendships become present/past instead of adjusting constantly from the present to the future. The Father is always present/future in His relationship with us (see Jer. 29:11).

Everyone needs to be re-envisioned as they grow up! Some leaders borrow vision from the good practice of other churches, but this seldom works as effectively as in the place of origin.

If the church in Sardis likes what the church in Philadelphia has done regarding vision/ministry and does the same thing in Sardis, it ceases to be the church in Sardis! It is now the church of Philadelphia in Sardis. The only thing it has done is borrow a model and try to make it fit in a different place. Models are not transferable; principles and values are! It is not just the location that is different. The history, sins, problems, warfare—all are different, as well as the culture, economics, and mind-sets. The people in your church are not the same. They have different personalities, experience, gift mix, anointing, families, jobs, responsibilities, time availability, finances, age range, and on and on! There are many differences, and those differences are crucial to the vision and ministry of your church.

In Southampton, United Kingdom, where I used to live, the city has centuries of ship and boat-building experience. The first question asked when a new boat is commissioned is: What sea will it sail in?

They look at navigational and weather charts for that region and then build a boat that can survive and prosper in that environment!

When we are considering a church plant, we examine the region and its problems, warfare, and the current needs, and then we develop a team to meet that specific challenge. The people whom God has given you are uniquely gifted to meet the needs of the people among whom God has placed you!

The vision is therefore drawn from the acute needs of the locality and the personality and giftedness of the people, and the power/purpose of the Holy Spirit. However, the vision you begin with is never the one that you will end with. It will change quite drastically.

Pioneering vision must always eventually give way to empowering vision. A pioneering vision is usually given to an individual/couple or a small team starting a work. They charge the atmosphere with vision, giving focus, direction, energy, and faith—often single-minded and dominant faith. God adds to these people with human resources, such as spiritual growth and finances.

The maximum time to serve someone else's vision is seven years. We see this fact in the story of Jacob and Laban (see Gen. 29). Jacob agreed to serve seven years in order to marry Rachel, his great love. Anyone who serves longer is almost certain to be cheated of something in the process. The issue here is that Jacob prospered within his serving, as all good servants will do. Then, a servant will need room and resources to grow in all that he or she is becoming in the Lord. After seven years, we must acknowledge that what God is doing in certain people is just as important as the corporate vision we serve. In fact, what God is doing is certain individuals may change the broader vision of the work.

Never underestimate the power and anointing that grows in a man and a woman who are wholeheartedly pursing the Lord. People who live a surrendered life have an impact on groups that are out of all proportion to the reputation.

When people and circumstances change, we must move from a point of familiarity to a place of inconvenience. Our previous comfort zone becomes a place of restriction.

Some things operationally may fall through the cracks. It's exceedingly difficult to continue with business as usual during a period of transition. It's like trying to keep appointments in an earthquake. When the landscape of your life is changing under your feet, it's probably a good idea to run with a different mind-set for a while!

In times of transition and major change, we must budget for failure. We have not passed this way before, and we need to lighten up on people. We are feeling our way, learning to walk in more sensitivity to the Holy Spirit. A mind-set does not change in a short period. It takes time, which cannot be allocated but only used wisely. We must develop better responses of obedience, intimacy, and faith. We need time to upgrade our relationships with the Father and one another.

As we have mentioned, pioneering vision must give way to an empowering one. People grow up and want to make a different contribution. They prosper, and receive a new anointing and fresh impartation. They are wiser, more mature. Therefore, a new relationship must develop. Vision must change to accommodate all that God has developed in the group.

The original vision must go into the ground and be rebirthed in people. Some of the same elements may return but in a different format. A process of reinvention occurs, and new partnerships emerge to get the job done.

A church experiences a vital stage of transition and vulnerability in order to rediscover vision and generate new partnerships. At this time, the original vision holders are reinvested at greater depth. The vision changes because the church realigns herself with a moving God.

Where the original vision holders are fathers and operate from a relational paradigm, the process of transition is not difficult. Relational leaders always anticipate the heart of the Father and have His passion for mentoring and releasing people. On the other hand, when the original vision holders operate from a functional paradigm, being task and purpose driven, then they are often more protective of their turf. Their original vision cannot be touched. If it is adjusted, it is always top down. They believe they are the sole arbiters of the vision and that God has brought people to the work to serve them.

Often, the result of that philosophy is a power struggle. When people are not empowered to discover their identity and pursue their destiny in Christ, then they are not being discipled but used. They are not sons being fathered, but servants being given a job to do. A pioneering church always works hard to establish a culture for personal growth.

Good leaders create environments where people learn to be sensitive to the Holy Spirit. Every believer must be living in the personal good of who they are in Christ, to learn to live by faith and walk in the truth by themselves. It is a New Testament requirement that each believer is able to hear the voice of God.

We need apostles and prophets to combine together to lay the foundations of the new Church that God is birthing through this period of transition. We need pastors and teachers to help build on the top of such supernatural input. If the Church does not make a place for all the fivefold giftings to operate both on a consultant and an operational basis, then we cannot rise to the required level of supernatural anointing that will create breakthroughs over our regions and cities.

In addition, we need other partnerships between prophets and teachers to further develop a life in the spirit, to enable people to hear prophetically, to know God's will, to develop authority and accountability, to nurture them into experience and a place of power, increasing faith and anointing.

We also need partnerships between evangelists and pastors so that we can align the people with the heart of God for the lost. If we are to reach a hurting world, we must learn the wisdom and power required to create an open heaven where we live.

It is a source of deep concern to me that churches do not tap into the wisdom and strategies that all true evangelists possess in order to reach our communities for Christ.

In the process, we disciple people to know their identity, calling, gift mix, and destiny. We mentor them into maturity by experience of God in life and ministry. The principle to learn here is the outworking of vision and corporate ministry is always adjusted through God's dealings with the individual.

People learn how to "stir up the gift" that is in them. It is interesting to note that most breakthroughs present themselves at inconvenient times and occur through mature people stirring themselves to believe the Lord. Yet it seems that many leaders spend a lot of time trying to stir up life in people. How many of our meetings revolve around motivating the saints instead of equipping them?

Chapter Two

DEVELOPMENT OF PEOPLE AND CHURCHES

T HERE are four stages of development that people grow through as they respond to mentoring. It is the same process for the corporate Body as it is for the individual.

These stages need only last to the point where we "get it," learn the lessons required, and make the adjustment.

INPUT

We need partnership of pastors with teachers to: take people into the process of salvation, understand the series of steps required to be saved, establish a lifestyle of repentance and truth, build doctrinal foundations that allow people to access and experience the Lord, and release people from bondage/history.

Our supernatural tools are baptism in water and the spirit, establishing the principles of relational Christianity—values and principles, developing cell group dynamics that are environmental, including pastoral cells for abused people, teaching cells for specific topics, and evangelistic cells for the purpose of mission.

People spend an appropriate season in specific cells being nurtured and then they pass into a different growth environment to develop gifting and experience of the Holy Spirit. In that context, they also learn how to cooperate and how to develop character and dependence upon God. For example, I train everyone regarding how to hear the voice of God, how to discern His will, and how to pray successfully! I train people in stillness, rest, waiting on God, and meditation. These are vital disciplines to a life of sensitivity to the person of God.

Currently, churches have too many maintenance ministries for church people. How many of your leaders and staff are mentoring, discipling, training, and releasing people? How many of the people in your church are not walking with God consistently? How many fail to respond to the Holy Spirit regularly? How many are unfamiliar with faith as a lifestyle? How many do not practice standing on the truth? How many are pushed around by the enemy and circumstances? How many have not settled the question of ownership, so the Lordship of Christ is in doubt?

The input stage is designed to encourage people to live by First Corinthians 6:19-20! My body is a temple of the Holy Spirit. I do not belong to myself but to God. I have been bought with a price; therefore, I want to glorify God in my life. Input is where we establish the culture of radical Christianity. The people who have developed commitment will be committed to their own development!

MONITORING

This involves two parallel activities. First, in our discipling of people, we must monitor their lifestyle. All relationships include accountability as soon as possible.

Accountability is not about controlling people but about enabling them to discover the freedom that exists in making wise choices. It is for freedom that Christ has set us free.

Accountability is about character development—learning to love the truth, learning to precede truth with grace and to follow it with mercy while enshrining it with love, patience, and kindness. These attributes of God taken together release the true reflection of God's glory—that He is good.

How we speak into people's lives will increase their revelation of God and enables intimacy to flourish. Alternatively, we may cause the opposite to occur. We must establish people in a place where they need the Holy Spirit rather than create a dependency on our ministry.

Monitoring is about changing mind-sets, perceptions, and language, regarding how people discern themselves, the Lord, and other people.

We must mentor people into faith and away from procrastination. People need to live in a place where their worship, praise, and prayer life are observable and inspirational to others.

In our development of people, it is so vital that we disciple them properly in terms of their experience and response to both Scripture and the Word of God. We can read Scripture and enjoy its insights, perceptions, and principles. This shared wisdom is knowledge that will help us on our journey with the Lord. However, we must use Scripture to develop a relationship with Christ, the Living Word.

It is essential here that our knowledge must give way to wisdom and revelation. Wisdom is the understanding of how God thinks about things, how He sees people and circumstances, and how He likes to do things.

Revelation occurs when wisdom penetrates our hearts to the point of transformation. We see, know, and therefore have an actual experience of the truth that changes our personality and how we act about something. Revelation is the Word becoming real in our experience of God. We become the truth that God has revealed; consequently, people around us will see that truth whenever they encounter us.

Without the input of the Holy Spirit, we take truth from the tree of knowledge of good and evil. Whereas, with Him in our life, we eat from the tree of life where relationship grows and we are radically changed.

As we learn to stand on the Word, the Spirit teaches us the amazing dynamics of confession, declaration, and proclamation. These disciplines of authority in the Word are what enable us to produce champions in the Spirit.

Monitoring is about giving people things to do. Assignments are at the heart of all ministry initiatives. If I travel to a particular city, church, or event, I am on a particular assignment for the duration of my visit. It may be to release a specific truth, speak to certain people, or establish a breakthrough in order to deliver a prophetic word.

People need to be engaged in team. As people are enfranchised to pursue the vision and call that the Lord has put on their heart, a whole raft of projects, ministries, and initiatives will be birthed both in the Kingdom and the church.

We can monitor the process of people's development, giving loving feedback and nurturing their faith and relationship with the Lord through the key pathways of mistakes, failure, learning, adjusting, becoming, and transforming.

Good mentors allow people to struggle before God in a way that guarantees growth.

SELF-GOVERNMENT

People must learn how to police their own lives well. A lot of leadership time can be wasted on policing things on behalf of others that they are not doing for themselves.

The only acceptable control in church life is the fruit of self-control that comes out of our ongoing relationship with the Holy Spirit. If people do not come to a place of self-government, then they must always be watched and seldom fully trusted. Honesty and integrity are only established through loving confrontation that seeks our highest good.

It is vital if we are to give truth to others that certain elements of truth-giving are in alignment. First, our own accountability must be clearly seen as operational and working effectively. As a rule, I will never make myself vulnerable to people of lesser character than myself. Nor am I happy to receive truth from someone when I cannot see any evidence of accountability in their own life.

If truth is not accompanied by grace, mercy, and above all love, then people will lack the patience, kindness, and goodness of God to release the whole person. In that context, necessary firmness becomes browbeating. People are hunted down and cornered by the issue, often being given no leeway to digest and process what they are receiving.

The object of truth is Jesus becoming real to the person we are mentoring. Truth must lead to an encounter with the love and personality of God. When we know what the Father wants to be for us, then we can submit wholeheartedly to His grace and goodness. But when people do not enable us to see Jesus, then we are forced to acquiesce to their ministry and their perception of truth. In that context, self-government is the goal and the focus of the exchange. However, self-government in itself can never be a goal; it is a consequence.

Jesus is the goal and focus of all that we do. He must have the preeminence in all things. When He is lifted up, He draws people to Himself. When people receive who He is for them within the issue or their struggle, there is a submission that arises out of the experience of being loved. Self-government is a consequence of the King of Love being revealed.

Accountability in its finest sense is not about submission. It's about the agreement to be righteous. It's about choosing ownership of Christ within the makeup of your own personality. Accountability is about people having the freedom to choose their own death. For example, when you choose holiness, you choose to kill a particular sin! Righteousness is present but can be obscured by sin. It is about a relationship that is geared to a personal discovery of truth and a release towards moral thinking about oneself. Accountability is also about having people face their potential, their identity, and their destiny.

When people have received major prophetic input, the next thing we must do after examining the Word is to talk about their own lifestyle. We must examine all the obstacles in the life of people that would prevent the word from coming to pass. It is vital in the context of pursuing the future that we come to a place of self-government so that our power and anointing are not compromised.

Prophecy talks about the possibility, not the inevitability, of fulfillment. All personal prophecy is conditional upon our response and our hunger for personal growth and transformation. People must understand the freedom that is available to them within their current circumstances.

We need both vertical and horizontal accountability—to God and man. If we are in charge of our own accountability, then we will never be honest enough to die properly and will either lose our freedom or not progress to the next level.

Self-government is also about developing a person's individual capacity for servanthood. A servant spirit must progress into stewardship. This is an intentional journey into a place of responsibility for others.

We learn to serve someone else's vision for a season while our own is developing. We learn about faithfulness, integrity, and hard work. We attain life disciplines. We discover the difference between commitment and convenience. Life interrupts ministry and vice versa. When we love from a place of commitment, we are prepared to be inconvenienced. Of course, the opposite of that is also true—people who are continual inconvenience to others by their actions or lifestyle, need to learn about consideration and commitment.

When we become excellent servants, we are promoted to stewardship. Our sense of God toward others needs to grow to a place of responsibility. Then we can partner with the Holy Spirit in a new way. We become realigned with the heart of the Father, not just His purpose. Part of our stewardship will involve mentoring others in the disciplines to which we have already surrendered, while an unsurrendered life has nothing to say.

Within our role as stewards, particularly of the grace of God, we are encouraged to develop our lives in a team concept. Mature partnerships with the Holy Spirit do not become fully fashioned outside of the human team dynamic.

MATURE PARTNERSHIPS

All relationships of long standing will need to go through several phases of reinvention. As we grow and become more, our identity begins to change. Therefore, we need to continually see one another in a proper new light that is compatible with their emerging distinctiveness.

Alongside their new identity, increased authority, and new persona, we must understand that their function will need some readjusting too! In this context, people may lose the grace for what they have been doing while having a longing for something new or different.

A natural part of transition is to negotiate change with likeminded people. Is it a matter of finding your successor in one place so that you can be training and exploring the next phase of your own development. Will the change necessitate a restructuring of your department or ministry? Will it require not just a change of personnel but also an adjustment in how we provide the service or the ministry?

It is vital in transition that we identify new roles and new people to fit them. By the term "new," I do not just mean totally new personnel, but to include those people in our midst who have or are becoming new in the change process.

Transition can give everyone a fresh start, a new identity, and a completely different release of life. God makes all things new; therefore, transition is about celebrating newness of life. Hopefully, we all are becoming new in the process so we can enjoy and sustain the level of excitement and encouragement needed to break through into a new place.

Mature partnerships emerge best when there is no hierarchy to prevent them. We must seek peer-level commitments as people grow and prosper to new levels. It is vital that we recognize growth in people and see it through to a proven place of faith, persistence, and durability. People must demonstrate their commitment and be dependable under attack. It is also essential that people coming into a place of leadership and ministry must be financially committed to the work of God that they represent.

The process is about turning servants into sons so that we can enjoy the paradox in relationship and ministry. Sons must be allowed to become fathers in their own right. This necessitates a shift in emphasis upon their heart and life.

Church, therefore, is a living, growing, organic entity that creates an environment for growth and change to occur. The early church was such a company of change agents, whereas the present church is often merely a refuge from change.

Following are some of the big questions in transition: How do we develop the church of today while still living under the routine and regime of the church of yesterday? How do we develop partnerships at a new level in our existing church situations when we have not developed the work from the beginning?

We may have inherited a people of mixed maturity with a limited understanding of the value and purpose of team. We may have no experience of building on values and principles. There may be personality clashes because ego is placed on a higher level than humility. We may have a situation because of past poor leadership where the disciplines of submission and obedience are seen as control and domination.

It is important to work with people who are able to move quickly and who see themselves as pioneers or initiators. These people are catalysts and will therefore help us to get transition off the ground and into some kind of momentum. The next group we work with are the enablers. These are good support people who, when trained can lend their spiritual weight, faithfulness, and strength that will energize and sustain the whole group into the right place of transformation.

These two groups together constitute the real power and anointing in the group. It is important that they are released into their role and place before we tackle the main problem in the church. This is our group of resistors. Every church has them. If they are a large part of your leadership, then you can forget becoming a new church. It simply will not happen. You can fight the battle, and then you can either pick up the pieces with a much reduced group numerically or simply leave and begin a work from scratch.

There are legitimate resistors who are newly saved people working through their baggage. These people, who are a necessary and important drain on our resources and time, are not able to offer much in the way of input and support. Then there are illegitimate resistors among us. These are people often with a nomadic church history who want you to take responsibility for their lives without giving you the authority to change anything. There are self-styled ministries who have an agenda to develop a platform for themselves but lack the character or integrity to develop one out of servanthood and humility. There are people who just want to "stay as we are," and who will resist change because it disturbs their comfort zone. For a more full description of these groups—initiators, enablers, and resistors—see my book, *Divine Confrontation...Birth Pangs of the New Church*, published by Destiny Image.

As leaders, we want to demonstrate grace and servant leadership, but we recognize we are dealing with unrefined personalities who need development as well as example. It's very important that our priorities are right and steadfast. We live and lead by principle and value. A team needs the mutuality of shared principles and values; otherwise, the team will collapse under pressure.

A servant heart is vital throughout the church. People are promoted to leadership and ministry on the basis of stewardship, not servanthood. A servant is someone willing to serve in the whatsoever/whosoever manner! A steward has a sense of responsibility to someone for someone and something.

Stewardship is primarily about the benefit of the people to whom you are called. Before dispensing authority and permission, check the life of the one being promoted. What is the witness of your spirit concerning their servant heart? Do you feel they are trustworthy? What is the evidence? Are they for you and the work you represent? Or are they simply building a platform for their own ministry?

The leader's role is to protect the flock and mentor people. People should be in ministry on mutually agreed terms, unless the moral integrity of the work is under threat; then, in areas of righteousness, holiness, and responsibility, leaders write the agenda.

Leading by principles and values can take the sting out of some issues that may be confrontational—for example, accusation of control, disempowerment, autocratic leadership, etc. Principles are deep fundamental truths that have a universal application. Principles are not values. A gang of thieves can share values but be in direct violation of the law.

Principles are objective and external. A principle describes the real territory of life and provides a compass heading for the journey. A compass always tells you where you are in relation to your travels.

Values are subjective and internal. A value represents our own internal alignment with the principle. It describes how we choose to act in regard to the principle.

For example, take the principle that God is good. His goodness is a huge part of His glory as Moses discovered (see Exod. 33:18-19). Do good to all men, especially those of the household of faith. One of my values that arise out of this principle is called divine advantage. This is where I seek the good of all those with whom I am in friendship with or with whom I do business. It is important to me that they receive an advantage/advancement in the relationship we develop.

A farmer has to work around the natural laws of the harvest, including preparing the ground, planting seed, watering, nurturing, weeding, and cultivating the plant before it can be harvested. All of these must be done at very specific times. A farmer has to work hand-in-hand with the process of creation.

Principles and values are always accompanied by process. We understand process in physical things. For example, a child must learn to turn over, sit up, crawl, stand, walk, run, jump, swim, etc. Each stage is important, and each step takes time. No step can be safely missed, though we can get through them at different speeds. A process cannot be violated without serious consequences. A process is a series of steps and stages that we navigate on our journey of transition.

Israel had to move from closure concerning Egypt, through conversion from a rabble of slaves to a disciplined army in the desert, in order to reach the point of being commissioned to take the Promised Land.

All major things in life come out of process. A company cannot succeed without the process of financial controls. There are rules of engagement in war and medical practice for surgery, to name but a few.

Part of the story of this book is concerned with the process of change. How do we get from this place to the next? Along the way we will make good decisions as well as take the opportunity to make better ones! When we do something for the first time, we inevitably learn how not to do it. Our first mistakes in a new process are more about the learning than the error. Failure to learn is the only real mistake we can make when doing something for the first time.

The journey of the Third-Day Church is a pioneering adventure. They will walk off their map and then make a new one as they follow the Holy Spirit. Theirs is a journey, a process of discovery, growth, and newness. Along the trail of their progress, we will find discarded ideas, pieces of vision that can never work. Their footprints will go down a few blind alleys and dead canyons. There will be some people in their wake who are excited about the concept of "third day" but who will fall out of love with the process and who are now journeying to find their real tribe.

It requires one step to start a journey. What will yours be?

Chapter Three

CHURCH AS A LIVING SYSTEM

An Organic and Organizational Paradox

SEVERAL hundred years ago Newton proposed a theory about organizational structure using the machine as a metaphor. If things don't work, we can replace the parts and carry on. Parts wear out and need replacing, but the system must continue to function.

This is at odds with the spiritual paradox in First Corinthians 3:5-16; 4:14-17. We talk in one breath about church planting and in another about organizational structure. We must live in both sides of the paradox to experience God. The church, just like a farmer's field, is concerned with organic life, while the church as a building represents organizational life.

In Scripture, we read about body parts, not machine parts. Each part has a function (see 1 Cor. 12:12-31). Each part deserves similar honor, and each part needs to be cared for. Body parts grow! Body parts change. And so, church needs a structure that is adaptable to growth and change.

A lot of church-growth teaching is only about putting structure into church; it's a mechanistic understanding that replaces people as they go wrong or cease to function properly in the system. The control factor is huge as we replace people in this way. People are ousted! People who don't fit the picture are squeezed until they do. When God shakes mechanistic structures, they fall down; when God shakes Kingdom relationships, they adjust to his heart.

God is a God of order, but He doesn't tell you what His order is! The wind blows where it will! Transactional leaders care for the structure, while transformational leaders care for the people. Church is organic and structured. The issue is primacy! We grow people organically and have a flexible structure to support the growth. Vines have a trellis. Trees have stakes.

ORGANIC CHURCHES

With organic church, constant growth requires a continuous adjustment of the structure (framework) of church. Structure serves the life. Organization supports the organic lifestyles we're developing in Christ. Choose people who are flexible and adaptable as your core team. Have workers serving in focused areas as a support team to aid the growth of the body. They may stay in one place of ministry, but their disciples will move on to other support relationships. Life outgrows its support system! All trees begin with a thin cane. As the tree grows, the length and strength of the support changes!

DNA is present in everyone and changes the flavor of the church. Yet a structure has no DNA, only a sense of order. This is why it is so vital that we move away from functional paradigm as the prime place where the church operates in life and ministry. A structure has no DNA! If you stake a tree, the DNA is in the tree, not the stake. As the tree grows, the support structure changes. The DNA in the tree causes life to emerge and a tree to grow! Churches that organize people cannot grow them to the level of power they need to break through personally.

Grow to the max of your DNA and make sure that growth is not hindered by the organizational structure. If you can't grow bigger, grow more! If you can grow a church only to 120, then give that one away to someone who can grow it more and plant another one, or plant some people elsewhere and help them grow. Become a mentor for start-up churches!

Grow to your full stature and keep planting. DNA is revealed through everyone to form the corporate life. Many churches today act as though only leaders and ministries have any DNA! Because that mind-set is prevalent, it means that we have developed a system that clones people into miniatures and caricatures of the superstars in the building!

You are God's field and building. The church is a living, creative, experimenting experience between people and their God. That experience leads us to discover God and what He has given to one another. It is impossible to build church without growing people! But in a functional paradigm, people are more aware of how the church works than they are the ways of God!

Organic and organizational is a wonderful paradox. We must live in the tension of both. Tension does not mean that something is wrong; it means that something is happening. But when organic and organization clash, it's time to change the structure. Unfortunately, a functional paradigm keeps the structure and gets rid of people who don't fit!

In Acts 27, Paul is sailing to Rome when a huge storm hits the ship. In the ensuing panic, every attempt is made to lighten the ship. It's a great metaphor for a church in the storm of transition—keep the people and get rid of the cargo. Take a critical look at the "stuff" you came on board with and decide if it will survive the process of transformation. Traditions, mind-sets, and irrelevant paradigms must all be tossed overboard as we major on keeping the people and causing them to grow in the Spirit and the purposes of God. The growth of people is always more important than the structural shape of the church.

We cannot sacrifice the individual for the system. Consequently, we must grow people before we put them into a structure. Then we must ensure that the structure is in tune with their identity, calling, and destiny; or it will break them. People must be broken in their relationship with God, not by a church system that cannot give them freedom.

LIVING SYSTEM

The church is a living system of intelligent, adaptable, creative, self-organizing, and meaning-seeking people, who may feel confined by something that should be releasing and empowering them to be the best they can be. Everyone hates to be confined. It destroys the soul and kills any initiative and creative desire.

Study any aspect of creation from insect to animals, fish to fowl, and humankind, and you will discover that all God's creation has a natural creative tendency to organize. However, everything for humans must be relational in context. Our task-oriented functions must stem from real friendships, or we cannot rise to our full DNA.

As we have received Christ Jesus the Lord, so walk in Him. We were presented with a relationship with Him, not an organization, having been firmly rooted and now being built up in Him and established in your faith, just as you were instructed and overflowing with gratitude (see Col. 2:6-7).

Next verse: See that no one takes you captive through philosophy and empty deception, according to the traditions of men, according to the elementary principles of the world, rather than according to Christ (Col. 2:8).

It's my contention that so much of the hierarchical and governmental principles of the world in business are now in use by the church. Yet organization should serve the life, not vice versa. We are supposed to be the answer to Paul's prayer in Ephesians 3:14-21!

For this reason I bow my knees to the Father of our Lord Jesus Christ, from whom the whole family in heaven and earth is named, that He would grant you, according to the riches of His glory, to be strengthened with might through His Spirit in the inner man, that Christ may dwell in your hearts through faith; that you, being rooted and grounded in love, may be able to comprehend with all the saints what is the width and length and depth and height—to know the love of Christ which passes knowledge; that you may be filled with all the fullness of God. Now to Him who is able to do exceeding abundantly above all that we ask or think, according to the power that works in us, to Him be glory in the church by Christ Jesus to all generations, forever and ever. Amen.

Only organic life can lead us into the width, length, height, and depth of God's love. Agape in a relational context is the bedrock for us to meet and function together. Without it, we are enslaved to something that will surely kill us or take away our meaning!

Life organizes around an identity which must be Christ, not church. Networks, patterns, and structures emerge quite naturally from those relationships. Acts 6:1-7 is a case in point! Leaders facilitate the joining of people together and help them explore how their friendship can glorify God. We set values and encourage vision and then support what emerges!

It is when structure originates outside that relational paradigm and is then imposed on organic life that we have an imposition that cannot reach its full potential. Life is attracted to order. Order arises out of exploring our relationships and the new possibilities that people bring.

Life gives constant invitation to freedom, which releases the creativity needed to explore in the Spirit. What we discover in this provides us with meaning that allows us to have a certain order that facilitates life!

CYCLES

It's a cycle. Order perpetuates freedom, which continuously releases creativity. Creativity encourages exploration, which always leads us to discovery. Discovery leads to meaning, which interprets life in the way that God plans for now! It's the law of life in Christ Jesus. It's the law of creation. The desire of every human being is to belong, to be loved, to be significant.

Order and organization are an essential part of our life cycle with God and one another, but they must be compelled by love, by relationship, and not by efficiency and economy. There is an effervescence in relationships that carries us into the anointing and the presence of God.

Why are we always asking God to come down and change the Church? It's because in our hearts we know He is not present in what the Church has become and we're not growing as we would like!

God is vague about organization structure but profound about life and relationships. Get together, support one another, and create (make it up as you go along)! Give each other freedom to love, relate, create; be significant and develop your own relational order to facilitate further exploration and discovery.

We are God's workmanship—"poema" (see Eph. 2:10). All of life in the church is based around the poetry of people loving and connecting together. A poem is a series of images that evoke an experience, linking things together for new ways of understanding and communication.

The search for significance must be earthed in real relationships, not just in a functional situation. If our only means of relating to the King and His Kingdom is through the establishing of a functional paradigm, then we have lost our incentive for real spiritual growth.

People will cling to their title, status, role, and position in order to maintain their grip on which they believe belongs to them and theirs. Order helps us discover what works. We keep changing, adapting, and creating as the life within and around us changes.

All life goes through cycles of change. How many changes have you gone through with your spouse? Friend ⇨ fiancé. Newlywed ⇨ Honeymoon period. Homemaker ⇨ pregnancy. Motherhood ⇨

young mom (toddlers). Mother/mom (older kids, college, just us two). Wife ⇨ Grandma. At least 12 cycles!

As life grows and changes, we become more creative and adaptive to release that life at different levels of belief and discovery. Everyone's significance changes as life grows, which creates a new order.

A single life has power to create. That's why God has given us imagination. Corporate life creates more! The Holy Spirit creates opportunities to discover God and be at work with Him in what He is creating. Even at inconvenient moments (consider Acts 10), God works, then invites us to be part of what He is doing. My Father works and I work.

Corporate life creates opportunities (if it's organic, it's continuous) because we know that in God there are endless possibilities. Functional church misses out on the inherent creativity of most of its people because most of them do not know they have power in the spirit to create.

That's where church as a stereotype is produced. On the other hand, a prototype church is an organic community loving life in God and one another. Organic and relational leaders create a cycle of belief that enables our identity to grow so that our relationships can improve so that we can change our environment. You are God's field and the Kingdom of Heaven is a seed falling into good soil and into indifferent soil. Buy the field because there is treasure in the hearts of God's people.

Without the life expression of an organic community, we will develop a logic and an institutional hierarchy based on function, not relationship. In this functional world, we build on rules, laws, and principles. In a relational world, we build on trust and values, plus principles. Principles tell us who we are. Values tell us how to handle relationships.

There is not one answer to something but many possibilities. Sometimes we are led specifically by God (consider Paul and Macedonia); other times we do what seems good to us and the Holy

Spirit. We carry on, being led together, and God specifically breaks in through prophecy, circumstances, and divine interventions. This is the way; walk in it! Enjoy the exploration, enjoy one another, and like Abraham trust God to get you there! (See Heb. 11:8.)

Modern day church is very Newtonian in its approach to life. A mechanistic mind-set sees people as objects to use to maintain order. Nonprophetic leadership can never see the Kingdom of God.

PROPHETIC LEADERSHIP

Prophetic leadership involves starting a think tank and anticipating the future. Nonprophetic leadership cannot invest in people who are outside their current norm or comfort zone. This type of order without the true prophetic grieves the Holy Spirit. A functional paradigm may allow people to prophesy but seeks to control the output. This is where establishment prophets are birthed rather than controlled.

The tragedy of much present-day evangelicalism is that it is earthed in a natural form of logic by leaders who have no prophetic insight but who do possess a power of veto. Every generation has a different cultural presentation. Nonprophetic leadership can only go so far in owning the future; it is more concerned with owning the present. Life in spirit is about now and not yet, where the church leadership has now and future people living in harmony. However, we often develop people but want them to fit into existing structures. How do we shape the future now while not controlling it? Through relationships and not a functional structure. Leadership must use the power of veto only in cases of immorality, disunity, and doctrinal clarity.

Producing sons, who can function with the Father out of relationship, is the goal of our endeavors. Otherwise, we produce servants who serve the leadership and the church. Mentoring creates accountability, self-control, and unselfishness which develop discipleship.

If we are not relationally inspired, we produce a system, a framework that must be protected. We become pharisaical by default, not design. People know more about how the church works than God.

Leaders should be fatherly relational facilitators who oversee this lifecycle. Our common values should prevent organizational dominance by any one person or group as we lead mutually respectful lives. One of our values at The Mission (my home church) is friendship and flexibility above structure.

Some people are very creative and others very organizational. Some are initiators, other enablers. Some folk are pioneers, other settlers. Some are about creators and others are refiners. Some are introverts and others are extroverts.

What makes these differences combine together and work effectively is relationship, values, and the fruit of the Spirit. It means that we create patterns and examples in people, not models of church life. Models are not transferable; while values and principles are international, cross-cultural, interracial, and eternal. What works in one place works in one place! If the church in Sardis likes what the church in Philadelphia is doing and creates that model, it is no longer the church in Sardis. It is the church of Philadelphia in Sardis. Each church is located in a specific place and must evolve a company of people to meet the needs of that particular community.

We plant teams that grow into church, and the mode of the church constantly changes as people grow. No model can sustain life unless it limits it first!

Values and principles that make a model work in one area when transferred to a different culture will first seek to relate to the pattern of what God is doing with this new group of people.

Dressmakers make a pattern before they make the dress. Apostles create new designs to produce new patterns according to the grace in the lives of the people they are working with in each location.

The Bible is highly relational. The language is one of family, friendship, and love mutually shared in the business of life. In his first letter to the Corinthian church, Paul calls them his beloved children (see 1 Cor. 4:14-17). His goal is not just to be a tutor, a trainer, or an itinerant preacher to them. He seeks a relationship that is more powerful and substantial—one of a father to his children.

The purpose of Jesus coming to earth was relational. He sought to bring many sons into glory. Paul followed in that heavenly tradition. He did not want to see Corinth become a nonrelational company of people. Fathers in the house create a relational atmosphere that produces sonship in Christ. These sons are mentored so that they can grow into real fathers who produce healthy sons.

An apostle is not just a person who produces sons; their real intention is to create new fathers. An apostle is the New Testament equivalent of the Old Testament patriarch. The Lord often described Himself as the God of Abraham, Isaac, and Jacob—grandfather, father, and son. There is a three-generational dimension to leadership in the Kingdom of God.

An apostle is not someone who sits on top of the pile with a network of churches or a team of ministries under them. They are primarily supernatural and patriarchal.

The goal of apostles is not chiefly to produce a network. That, by itself, would be evidence of a functional paradigm at work instead of a relational one. We need both relationship and function together in order to grow and build. The relational aspect is always precedence in the heart of God. So we build relationships of worth and value, which have an agenda to build the Kingdom through loving community and mission. Our functionality is earthed in a relational context that seeks the good of people.

When networks operate solely out of function, they become empirical. This empire spirit is the antithesis of the Kingdom. It is man building something and using people to further an idea, a design that can never realize the presence of God. The Father looks for a habitation in which to live amongst His people. He seeks a relational company where He can relate.

A church operating mainly out of functional paradigm cannot experience God in that way. Task-driven relationships do not excite the Lord. He looks for love at a much deeper level. Functional churches may receive a visitation from time to time but not the continuous presence of the Lord.

The goal of apostles is to facilitate the Kingdom and to recognize that we have in our DNA the capacity to produce sons and turn them into fathers. All real apostles are challenged on the issue of Kingdom and network. What has primacy, and what does that look like at crunch time? The whole point of networking must be to learn how to grow people and how to use structures in the process.

If we have failed to establish the wider Kingdom principle in our network—chiefly, that "other churches matter"—then we have built something elitist and exclusive. If we have failed to build our ministry into a relational context that seeks the presence of God and the growth and good of people as tangible outcomes, then we have forfeited the creation of a habitation for God.

Rather, what we have established is a work that eventually must go into the ground and die so that the true Kingdom anointing can go to a higher level.

The reason why several networks have failed in the past 30 years is that they outstayed their welcome, they outlived their welcome, and they outlived their usefulness. When we need rules and bylaws to keep people and control their behavior, we do not have an organization built on relationship that seeks to grow sons into fathers. Instead, we have created a system that can only contain and never fully release people. It mistrusts people who do not fit. It promotes people who toe the line. It produces establishment people for the purpose of maintaining the structure. The scaffolding has become more important than the building.

The Third-Day Church has taken note of that error. This Church seeks a relational context that is able to fully function out of loving friendships of shared vision and faith. They understand that life is organic, and that within the DNA of all created life is the ability to self-organize for the purpose of growing and spreading. They know that even when church is built on the foundation of evangelist, pastor, and teacher, we cannot rise to a supernatural level becoming a world-beating community that lives in the favor of God.

Jesus must be allowed to set leaders free from the money game, the power game, the numbers game, and the prestige game. People deserve better than what they are currently getting from their churches.

The Third-Day Church has found a way forward that is commensurate with their DNA. They are relational in design, very permission-giving, and seek to enable their people to live in the dream that God has for every living soul. This book contains many of the principles and values they are discovering on their journey into the Kingdom and freedom.

Section Two

THIRD-DAY WORSHIP

Chapter Four

GOD-CENTRIC WORSHIP

THIRD-DAY gatherings are God-consumed. The whole genesis of "third day" is about a newborn, newfound freedom in God and with God. So the essence of a third-day gathering is to anticipate and experience that new freedom—a refreshed and renewed (not refurbished) freedom, a freedom from the conventional man-managed restraints of the Second-Day Church, a freedom to return the church's ownership to its founder, a freedom to restore God at center stage in His own house, and a freedom of resurrection to redeem and release a new generation of gatherings for the King.

Because of this new freedom, these new third-day gatherings are God-consumed. If there is anything distinctly different about these new expressions, as opposed to the predictable church gatherings of the past, it is that they are conspicuously for God, and not for people. They are not designed for the people in the pew, or for the people whom the church is trying to attract. They are for Him—to attract Him, to invite and draw and woo and please the Father.

They are "God-centric," not "Sunday-centric" or even "meeting-centric." It is worship; not preaching, or teaching, or evangelizing, or even our need for fellowship that is the inseparable mark of the church. Let everything else we do give way to our most prestigious call to worship the King.

For years we have called them "worship services." At least that is what is printed on the front of the bulletin that is handed to us each week at the front door. That is what it says on the sign out front where we change the cute little one-liners each week. But, knowing what we know about them, wouldn't it be better suited to advertise them as "preaching services," or "teaching times," or even just "Sunday services"?

What percentage of the average worship service, in actuality, is given totally to the worship of God? It has been said that 80 percent of all our time, energy, and money is spent making the flagship weekend services happen. What is the result? How much of the main meeting is actually given to the "pure worship" of God? And, I wonder who will be held ultimately responsible for our systems that actually keep people from His presence, rather than help usher them into it?

CAN THE NATIONS DRAW NEAR?

Much of my early understanding of Christ's purging of the Temple courts during the final days of His Passion week was based upon a fairly rigid view that pointed to the issue of Christ's anger being released towards the manipulative commercialization around the Temple grounds. I always thought His anger was unleashed at those "money changers" because of their greed and their intrusive marketing, their lust for filthy lucre...right?

History sheds light on the possibility that the bigger issue may not have been what these merchants were doing, as much as the space they were occupying. Could it be that they may have actually been providing a necessary service to the weary travelers on their way to the Temple as they provided a whole gamut of sacrifice options to meet the families' needs?

Mark's rendering, unlike the ones in Matthew or Luke, includes Christ's mention of His desire that access be given to all nations coming to this house of prayer. *"My house shall be called a house of prayer for all nations"* (Mark 11:17). So, how do the nations get in, if they cannot even get near?

With reserved and designated areas of access for the nations around the Temple being overrun by the "blue-light specials" of the sacrifice "flavor of the day," how could the nations even get near enough to see and hear the worship of God? Could it have been that the issue that touched our Lord's core and released such an unprecedented display of emotion was not just the merchants hawking their wares, as much as it was that Jesus felt driven to relocate them, to get their tables and kiosks out of the way, so that all the nations could get near. The question Jesus was rhetorically asking was, "Whose house is it?" It seems that whenever it stops feeling like the Father's house, and starts feeling and acting like someone else's house, a therapeutic cleansing is necessary.

How much of what we deem important and determine to do week after week in our worship services is actually preventing people from entering into worship and experiencing God's manifest presence in a significant, life-changing way? Are we inviting people to His house or ours? How much of what we think is essential to the corporate worship experience is no longer tenable and is actually getting in the way of His worship?

OUR HIGHEST CALLING

So to begin with, a third-day regional meeting is built on the belief system that the worship of God is our highest calling—that the uninhibited, unlimited worship of God, rather than of our sermons, agendas, schedules, or our programs, is the high point of these new "worship gatherings."

It means giving our meetings over to new ways of worshiping, new ways of praying, new ways of interacting to create new ways of lingering in the presence of God. It means that we no longer use the worship portion of the meeting, whether that be the first four worship choruses, or the choir specials, as some prelude, or "opening act" to set the "mood" for the sermon. It means that if we are going to call it a "worship service," then that is what it is—mainly worship.

Graham Cooke notes in his book *Divine Confrontation* that "Among churches today we have two kinds of worship: Synagogue and temple. Synagogue worship occurs when people come to church to hear the Word of God, receive ministry, and be entertained. It represents the doing aspect of body worship. Often, because the main reason for meeting is actually people-centered rather than God-focused, this worship is usually restricted when time is pressing. In temple worship, however, people come to praise God, to pray, and to make an offering. Their sole concern is for God Himself."[1]

Are we really ready to entertain the presence of God by adjusting our worship meetings to "host the Ghost"? Are we after the cloud and not the crowd? Are we ready for a shift in values about the amount of time we give for the worship that pleases the Father, rather than for a meeting that is ultimately captive to the clock?

PERSONAL INVASION OF THE KING

Many of us know what it is like, on a personal level, to be invaded by God's glorious presence in our daily, ordinary routines. Like Jacob, trying to catch a few winks with a rock for a pillow, God shows up, with His angels ascending and descending, and we find ourselves saying, "Surely the Lord is in this place, and I did not know it...how awesome is this place! This is none other than the house of God, and this is the gate of heaven." Instantly, our workplaces, our bedrooms, our living rooms, and our vehicles become our "Beth-els" (see Gen. 28:10-17).

In this season of God's visitation, we are finding ourselves faced with a renewed awareness of Emmanuel, "God with us," His "numinous" or manifest presence in our meetings. So, what do we do when He shows up? Well, far too often, that depends on what we feel must happen next in the meeting, or what kind of time press we are in, or whether a longer meeting might offend the visitors, or worse, the board of trustees. And yet do we ever consider the possibility that abruptly aborting the flow of a given "worship gathering" might actually offend God?

As evangelicals, we have understood for generations the protocol to God's presence. He dwells in the praises of His people (see Ps. 22:3). The question is: How do we conduct ourselves once we find ourselves in the presence of the King?

Jesus taught us to pray, *"On earth as it is in Heaven"* (Matt. 6:10b). So, what is going on in Heaven? Revelation 1:6 states that He has made us "all" to be priests to serve Him, while Peter says that *"you also, as living stones, are being built up a spiritual house, a holy priesthood, to offer up spiritual sacrifices acceptable to God through Jesus Christ"* (1 Pet. 2:5). What is the role of the priest? If what the Hebrew writer states is true, that *"every high priest taken from among men is appointed for men in things pertaining to God, that he may offer both gifts and sacrifices for sins"* (Heb. 5:1), then this priestly role of both worship and intercession is our way of opening a window into the very throne room of God! Remember, *"On earth as it is in Heaven."*

PRIESTLY WORSHIP REVEALED

What does this priestly worship look like? Quite simply, it looks like a lot of worship mingled with a lot of prayer. *"Then He came and took the scroll out of the right hand of Him who sat on the throne. Now when He had taken the scroll, the four living creatures and the twenty-four elders fell down before the Lamb, each having a harp, and golden bowls full of incense, which are the prayers of the saints"* (Rev. 5:7-8). It seems that prayer and praise are uniquely interrelated and were never intended to be separated. Psalm 141:2 reflects this marriage of worship and intercession when David prays, *"Let my prayer be set before You as incense, the lifting of my hands as the evening sacrifice."* So what we end up with is worshiping prayers and praying worshipers in the same gathering. What a concept! At the end of Psalm 72, in verse 20, it states, *"The prayers of David the son of Jesse are ended."*

Funny, I always thought these all were psalms or songs, not prayers! Jesus, in Matthew 21, Mark 11, and Luke 19, when He cleanses out the courtyard of the Temple, quotes Isaiah 56:7 and says, *"For My house shall be called a house of prayer for all nations."* He uses the Greek word, *proseuche*, from which we get our English word "prose." When translated, *proseuche* means unrhymed poetry. These poems can be put to melody, or the prayers turned into songs. It is here that we find a deliberate, significant, and effective way of sustaining the flow of His manifest presence in our worship gatherings.

GOING WITH THE FLOW

When we are willing to move beyond the staged performances of a few rehearsed songs led by a professional band, and into meetings where all believers begin to participate in more integrated forms of worship, something shifts. When our gatherings include spontaneous songs, prayers, intercession, prophetic words, etc., calling onlookers to become participants, something happens. Suddenly, an atmosphere is created where God is free to speak in the midst of the meeting, not just through the limited elite, and not only for the building up and edifying of the Church, but also for the purpose of actually engaging us in the meeting and interactive worship to giving specific direction to the meeting itself.

When this kind of release comes, everything changes. Worship changes, participation levels change, attention spans change. The meeting moves from the predictable routine to an orchestrated symphony, with God as conductor, writing the songs and scoring the music as we go along. Each meeting becomes different, unique, and alive with the people of God functioning as the priests of God, and not just as consumers.

Worship and intercession are uniquely interrelated, and their combined effect is greater than just one by itself. When this blended recipe of worship and intercession is released, and the Body is released to find key roles in the meetings, the saints are edified and God is glorified. We personally began our steps into third-day worship gatherings by allowing our prayer meetings to be invaded by worship, and our worship services to be invaded by prayers. There may be other things we will do in these meetings, but it all will come through a flexibility as God is allowed to orchestrate the flow, purpose, and impact of each meeting.

After all, these meetings are for Him, aren't they?

ENDNOTE

1. Graham Cooke, *A Divine Confrontation* (Shippensburg, PA: Destiny Image Publishers, 1999), 82-83.

Chapter Five

THE WORSHIP FEAST

WHEN we began to respond to this reformation, we could hardly have predicted what kind of "wild ride" this would ultimately be, particularly in its impact on our already radical gatherings. We were your typical Hawaiian-shirt, Bermuda-shorts, "laid-back" Southern California beach church, maintaining deep evangelical roots with evident Pentecostal, charismatic overtones. Our critics had already labeled us "different," "tribal," even "extreme" in our worship. But nothing in our past could have prepared us for the journey upon which we were about to embark.

Initially, we knew little to nothing of the prophetic implications of what was happening. As we went along, we discovered a new fervor. The temperature of God continued to increase when we gathered and worshipped Him. And as we hungered for more of God, we pressed into experiencing more and more of His manifest presence. Our meetings grew in intensity, in participation level, and obviously in length.

Some of our initial reactions required minor adjustments. But, after a while, we all knew that something very historic was happening—something so drastic that we had to face both legitimate concerns as well as direct opposition, and face them head-on. God gave us great grace. We made many attempts to respond to deliberate concerns about the changes we were experiencing. Many of these concerns deserved very honest answers. As the many questions came, the answers evolved. Some answers were quickly accepted; others were not so readily received. And along the way we also learned that it was both hard, and as well unnecessary, to "defend" God. Like Aslan, He is kind, but He is not safe!

WORSHIP IN THE WESTERN WORLD

Most of the "worship wars" these days range from battles over preferred volume, different kinds of instrumentation, and the many stylized techniques of worship leaders trying to accommodate someone's taste, usually the senior pastor's. But when it is all said and done, the real issue or real war is whether there is room in our corporate gatherings for the fervent, passionate worship of God Himself.

Rather than fixating on the methods of worship we use, the instrumentation, the sound, the sound system, the players, the mix, what about the real issues of the heart? What about concentrating on whether we have created an atmosphere where genuine expressions of our love and devotion to Abba, our Father, are actually honored and encouraged? In these days of the restoration of worship, we are being wooed back to Edenic parameters where the first man walked and talked in unabashed intimacy with his Creator. Deep and passionate worship tugs at us for response.

It is now time to confront the internal and external levels of resistance that keep us from this wholehearted lovemaking to Jesus, and to face the cultural taboos that have taken precedence over the passionate, expressive, responsive worship of King Jesus. So many of these cultural distractions have often been given free reign to compete with the allegiance that belongs only to our Bridegroom.

Mike Bickle, Director of IHOP (International House of Prayer), a 24-hour-a-day intercession ministry in Kansas City has said for years, "We are at a critical point in history. Right now, the Holy Spirit is wooing His Church. As God woos His Church, He is transforming it. He is making us a passionate, transcendent, power-filled body of believers. And, we crave the encounter we get when we experience Jesus as the passionate Bridegroom God who feels so deeply toward us."[1]

What do we do when the habits of our heart are being challenged? What do we do when the ways in which we have worshiped for years, even generations, are no longer in sync and are in direct conflict with what the Father is asking of us? What do we do with our precision-timed microwave meetings that can't possibly be allowed to run any longer than the average sitcom, while our Lover God is beckoning us to linger in His presence?

What do we do with the small children, who for years have been sent off to ten-by-ten foot cubicles to avoid any contact with the adult "real church" when these little guys are actually longing to lead us, the big guys, into "perfected" praise and worship (see Matt. 21:16)? What do we do when God chooses to ignore our bulletins, bypass our liturgies, and overrule our strategically placed wall clocks, and insists on taking us deeper into His secret place? What do we do when our own insatiable capacity for the manifest presence of God is too often left unsatisfied, unfulfilled, and even empty in our predictable worship regimens?

"BUT, THE SERVICES ARE TOO LONG!"

Nothing so readily reveals our cultural mind-set and our corporate experience of worship any quicker than the American standards we have set for the length of the average worship service. It has been researched that the first impact of renewal or refreshing or reformation on a local church is its affect on the structure, namely its direct impact on the normal church meeting schedule.

I was raised in a somewhat rural community, and we were unashamedly Pentecostal in our worship and desire to let God's Spirit move. But, let the Sunday service go too far past the sacred noon hour, and you could rest assure, expect, or know that someone's roast in the oven was turning into a "burnt sacrifice." It has always been amazing to me how we can easily watch a two or three-hour movie, add dinner, coffee, and dessert to the evening out, and have no second thoughts. Even though it may take four or five costly hours to complete, it is considered an evening well spent. From sporting events to concerts, all of these things take time to enjoy. Why not then allow the Lord some extended, prolonged, open worship?

Here are two key principles for this new worship:

1. Pace yourself spiritually. Rely on God's strength as you "wait" on Him, listening to Him to lead you in worship.

2. Pace yourself physically. You don't have to stand or dance or hold up your hands for the whole meeting. I'll never forget the day I talked to a brother before a worship gathering began. He was bending, squatting, and pulling in the back of this old bar where we were meeting. When I asked what he was doing, he responded, "This is the first church I have ever attended that I have to stretch before worship so I don't pull a hamstring!"

Ask God for wisdom as He shows you how you can ready yourself for a myriad of postures and responses to Him in your praise and worship: kneeling, bowing, laying prostrate, dancing, leaping, sitting. Learn to enjoy lingering in His presence, allowing Him to give you moment-by-moment direction on how He desires to be worshiped. And prepare both your heart and your body for the adventure.

"BUT, WHAT ABOUT SMALL CHILDREN?"

If you bring small children to these extended regional worship experiences, come prepared to help them enjoy the full worship experience, with their short, wiggly attention span and all.

1. Bring coloring books with crayons for them, or their favorite books to read. Bring them "temple bags," with snacks, small quiet toys, or games they can play.

2. At times during worship, engage with them directly and intentionally to join you, or better yet, you join them in the worship expression that is on their hearts.

3. Be with them in the meetings, holding them, walking with them, and dancing with them, connecting with them in their worship of God.

4. When the mood or move of the Spirit shifts in a meeting, use these opportunities as "teaching moments," giving them time for reflection and interaction on what God is doing. Ask them questions. Then respond to their answers.

5. Seek feedback from them when there is a prophetic word or prophetic song or dance. Let variety have its work in them and in you as you worship with them.

6. Work on new ways to engage your children during the meetings. For most it will mean an important shift from a lecture-only style of communicating to forms of getting the message across that allows and facilitates interaction, even with eight year olds.

7. Above all, let's train a whole new generation of kids to have passion and focus on the things of God and the things of the Spirit. Let's challenge them to be more excited about Jesus rather than their iPod, X-Box, or skateboard.

"BUT, I'M NOT A DANCER OR A SHOUTER!"

It is not about a certain style of worship or form or manifestation or expression that determines whether God is being wholeheartedly, extravagantly worshiped. Worship is to be God-ward, not man-ward.

So, we must try, especially in corporate worship, to get our eyes of comparison off others and discover how the Father wants us to worship Him.

Above all, be congruent in your physical actions with what is going on in your heart, and what God is requesting of you. It is blatantly incongruent, inauthentic, and ingenuous to move into outward expressions of worship simply because others are doing it, when you are instead being drawn into a more contemplative, silent, or serene place in your worship before God.

But, it is just as insincere to be contemplative or silent or serene, when in your heart you feel like dancing and leaping and praising God. I developed a great foundation for total wholehearted worship in my early days with John Wimber. I clearly got the idea that most of the Western world had a paradigm of worship that fostered a "split personality" that still permeates so much of American evangelicalism.

The Bible has a Hebrew view of man, not a Greek view with which we have bought into a worldview made explicit by the ancient philosopher Plato, which splits reality up like bifocals, or even trifocals. This "Platonic Dualism," as it has been described, causes us to devalue the physical expressions of worship in order to appear spiritual. And this fragmented worldview leads to distortion that affects our whole worship experience.

The Hebrew mind-set views man as a unity, while the Greek perspective analyzes man as a combination of body and soul (the material from the nonmaterial), or even body, soul, and spirit (physical, mental, spiritual).

The Hebrew picture neither splits man into two (dichotomous) or three (tricholomous) parts, but sees man as a unity with inner and outer dimensions. It sees the body as the physical expression or outward extension of the spirit or the "inner man." So when the whole man worships, he worships with a congruence that allows for an inward release and an outward expression that encompasses the kind of worship that Jesus said that the Father is seeking in John 4:23.

God is looking for complete, heartfelt, full-body worship that captures everything about us—spirit, emotion, and body. Worship becomes religious when we refuse to be fully ushered into new, all-consuming places in His presence—new places that He is inviting us to enter, even if those new places require more of us.

So, don't hide in your personal reservations when God wants you to burst out in dance or celebration. So many of the Hebrew words for worship are, in themselves, "illustrated action pictures." Like the Hebrew word for "rejoice" in Psalm 118:24, *"This is the day the Lord has made; we will rejoice and be glad in it."* The word "rejoice" in this verse is *guyl*, or *guwl*. It means "to spin around under the influence of violent emotion."

God is calling for wholehearted, whole-bodied, authentic worship. We don't worship worship, nor are we to be limited by our cultural standards or limitations. We worship Him. If He says "rejoice," then we dance violently.

A LIFESTYLE OF WORSHIP

Worship is about pure obedience to Him. He is the one who is leading, and He will call us to many new ways, new steps, and new turns in our worship experience. So what part of your anatomy does He not have full and complete access to? Your feet? Your arms? Your hands? Your head? It's all His, and He wants it all (see Rom. 12:1-2).

The Bible gives far more importance to the human body than most of us have been taught. It is viewed with dignity and is really quite inseparable from one's essential person. It is never viewed as an unnecessary addendum to the spirit. Man is not a pure spirit like God. He is, and always will be, a body person. He is so much so, that in the resurrection, it states in First Corinthians 15, *"if the body is not raised, nothing is left."* So in worship, give Him everything, every part of your being.

And finally, remember that these larger worship gatherings so common to our brand of weekend Christianity cannot be your only worship experience. What about your private times with God where it is just you and Him? Calvin Miller in *Table of Inwardness*, says of this worship encounter, *"Thou preparest a table before me* (Psalm 23:5)," and that there are only two chairs at the table, and there, we may sit and sup with the Son of God.[2]

I have personally experienced that it is hard to sustain stamina of worship in a corporate setting unless you have a worship foundation in you private times with God. Worship really is a "table set for two."

We are called to be worshipers as a lifestyle, not just in meetings. So, whether the issue is length of service, small children, worship style, or whatever, it must be about Him. It is about the worship that pleases Him. It is about the worship that He is seeking (see John 4:23). It is about the worship that He is worthy of. It's about worship that delights Him.

ENDNOTES

1. Mike Bickle, *The Relevant Church* (Orlando, FL: Relevant Books, 2005), 60.

2. Calvin Miller, *The Table Of Inwardness* (Downers Grove, IL: InterVarsity Press, 1984), 26.

Section Three

THIRD-DAY MEETINGS

Chapter Six

MEETINGS OF THE THIRD KIND

HOW many individual Christians do you know live with the haunting memory of wasted years, frozen dreams, and a disquieted passion? It is like a plague of despair throughout the Body of Christ as gifted, called, and visionary people struggle their whole lives with misplaced priorities and dashed destinies.

I believe that a major focus of the apostolic ministry these days has to do with helping individual believers discover who they are and what they have been called to do; then, for these same fathers to become the biggest fans of the army of God as they cheer, watch, and nurture children of God so that these believers are energized to excel and enjoy their place in the Son! In the same way that secure fathers create environs where their children flourish, apostolic fathers create an environment for gifting and calling, discovery, exploration, and fulfillment. One generation calls out the leaders in the next generation, and so on, and so on, and so on.

But, where does this freedom come from in a church world known for insecure and threatened leaders, who, in their own struggles or search for significance, often thwart others from doing much more than a token sideline or armchair ministry?

For most of my almost 40 years of public ministry, I have observed and operated in the only model I knew—that of the called, anointed, ordained, released, busy, many-gifted, jack-of-all-trades pastor upon whose shoulders lay the full responsibility for everything that happens in a local parish, and particularly, what happens in the all-important flagship Sunday worship service. Yet I knew that there had to be more to church life than the abysmal fruit of worn-out, burnt-out leaders and a passive priesthood in the pew.

MISSION: PERMISSIONAL

The rising apostolic church is not about more control, more hierarchy, or more systems of oppression. It is about the cultivation of a permissive missions-oriented atmosphere where everyone thrives, everyone grows, everyone dreams. The concept of the apostolic Third-Day Church is that everyone is on a mission. Surrounded by permission-giving leaders, they get to fulfill their mission.

Leaders become permissional and missional when they:

1) Become less purpose-driven and more dream-sensitive.
2) Create an atmosphere of inquiry rather than one where questions are stifled.
3) Help others "color outside the lines" rather than looking for prefabricated performances.

Permission-giving that releases others, particularly the less-trained and less-tenured, is difficult to embrace for many church leaders who have struggled through their own ministry-proving systems. Our early church fathers looked for those "full of the Holy Ghost," rather than those with the highest GPA from the most prestigious training center. They depended on the art of equipping rather than the matriculation of education. As a result, discipleship in the New Testament is seen as more of a transformational paradigm than an informational one.

When the Spirit falls among us, which was prophesied in Joel 2 and explained in Acts 2, dreams, visions, and prophecies are given to the old and the young, to men and to women, to boys and to girls, to the bond and to the free. Doesn't it make sense then, that in the purest form of cooperation with the Spirit's moving, that we enroll everyone upon whom the Spirit is falling? Not just allowing, but encouraging all Spirit-filled people to participate in significant ministry, and not just some token crowd response?

EVERYONE PLAYS!

This means addressing the "class system" that too often exists in today's church, with the leaders as the few, and the untrained as the many. Even though all are able to hear from God, most of our default systems return to the few leading the many.

A quick read of First Corinthians 14 shows us an environment where everybody gets to "do the stuff," where everybody gets "to play"—not just one person, or even an elite or select few people who are teaching, prophesying, or exhorting all the time.

It seems, at least from Paul's vantage point, that the essence of spiritual gifts is that they are always being passed along. Or as a contemporary movie noted, we take these acts and, "Pay It Forward." You get from God and give it away to another. The gifts come from Him, and you are the conduit, you are the pipeline, you are the vessel through which the gifts of God flow to the benefit or "profit" of all (see 1 Cor. 12:7).

First Corinthians 14:26 conveys this idea that when the church comes together, it follows an expression that has to, by its very nature, include more than just a few professionals. "How is it then, brethren? Whenever you come together, each of you has a psalm, has a teaching, has a tongue, has a revelation, has an interpretation. Let all things be done for edification."

I know how people have criticized the current usage of this passage, as though we all have looked for, hunted for, or longed for this as a pet text, a new reformational mantra, or a special elite handle for the open-type meetings we are encouraging.

So, let's set the record straight! This is not a prescriptive; it is not a directive! Paul is not saying that when you get together you must always do this. Neither is he saying that this is how each gathering of the church should function, with some set sequence of these expressions as being the newest, the latest, and the hottest way to do church.

This is really more of a responsive, or as someone described, a narrative. It is like Paul is saying, "Hey, I hear when you guys get together in the church in California, that many participate in the meetings. One sings, one teaches, one exhorts, one prophesies.... Well, whatever part you play, whatever it is that you feel God has called you to contribute to the gathering, just make sure everybody gets edified."

It becomes even more freeing or exciting when the word of encouragement comes through someone quoting a Scripture, or singing a song that they have written. What if someone wants to express their gift through a video presentation or the design of a flag? What if someone else choreographs a dance, illustrates a spontaneous sermon, or performs a rap around a biblical theme?

SIGNS OF LIFE

The key here is that in these gatherings more than one person can participate and that everybody needs to get edified. These meetings should always end up with the participants being delighted and the body as a whole being built up. It is like the overall function of the prophetic as mentioned in First Corinthians 14:3: *"He who prophesies speaks edification and exhortation and comfort to men."*

Does this happen in the stare-at-the-back-of-the-head-in-front-of-you-and-watch-the-professional-working model of today's typical church? Or is it back to the one-man band played by the octopus-type guy with cymbals on his knees, a harmonica stuffed in his mouth while he plays drums and an accordian with each arm? However we cut it, the same pattern of church for 500-plus years continues to be front and center in our showrooms. This pattern has the professional pastor talking and everyone else listening.

Rather than continuing to feed a system of meetings, which engenders gobs of spectators and tolerates a few worn-out participators, let's expend some of our creative energies and experiment with some venues that support the potential of everyone getting involved in the meetings.

With so many "one another's" in Scripture, we have our work cut out for us.

- Love one another (see John 13:34-35).
- Be devoted to one another (see Rom. 12:10).
- Honor one another above yourselves (see Rom. 12:10).
- Live in harmony with one another (see Rom. 12:16).
- Stop passing judgment on one another (see Rom. 14:13).
- Edify one another (see Rom. 14:19).
- Instruct (admonish) one another (see Rom. 15:14).
- Accept one another (see Rom. 15:7).
- Have concern for one another (see 1 Cor. 12:25).
- Carry one another's burdens (see Gal. 6:2).
- Forgive one another (see Eph. 4:32).
- Submit to one another (see Eph. 5:21).
- Agree with one another (see Phil. 4:2).
- Teach one another (see Col. 3:16).
- Encourage one another (see 1 Thess. 4:18).
- Build each other up (see 1 Thess. 5:11).
- Live in peace with one another (see 1 Thess. 5:13).
- Be kind to each other (see 1 Thess. 5:15).

- Encourage one another (see Heb. 3:13).
- Spur one another toward good deeds (see Heb. 10:24).
- Confess sins to one another (see James 5:16).
- Offer hospitality to one another (see 1 Pet. 4:9).
- Serve each other (see 1 Pet. 4:10).
- Show humility to one another (see 1 Pet. 5:5).
- Fellowship with one another (see 1 John 1).

SAINTS AMONG US

What can we do so that the "one another" ministry God has called the Church to is accomplished? How do we make room for these? You can begin by changing meeting configurations, adjusting meeting formats, even rescheduling meeting times, and procuring sites in different places that reinforce your values of doing relational, participatory church.

And for those who are not ready to give up their 30 minutes of singing songs and their 45-minute sermons, at least start to think outside the limited fast-food menu of your local burger joint.

Don't be satisfied to release just small portions or rations of the meetings to some token kind of participatory. Get bold, ask for some testimonies, and assign others to share parts of meeting for the day. Prepare your sermon outline around some questions and answers, always looking to draw others out in the meetings.

Experiment with formats of creative interaction where the priesthood and the prophethood of believers actually function. Do some things that affirm and bless the renewed saints movement that is among us these days, where the "each one" and the "everyone" gets to function fully in this arising, apostolic, Third-Day, virtual Church.

Chapter Seven

EMBRACING THE UNPREDICTABLE

WHEN you start doing "virtual church," church where all the gathered believers can potentially participate in the gatherings, things can get a little scary. But, as frightening as the possibilities may seem, it is something that has to be done. In the final analysis, instead of a single-pastor system with program-driven worship, each person in the Body is supposed to bring something from the Lord that will cause another to mature in love and good deeds.

Can the typical 45-minute sermon do that? I don't know. I think it can, maybe, do some of it. But I honestly doubt that it is fully adequate concerning the complex needs of the average congregation these days. And if the level of ministry is really happening where the people of God are carrying their gifts, their insights, their words, and sharing them in the church meeting, the meetings will become totally different than the ones where we rely solely on the preplanned homilies of the seminarians.

I know what you are thinking—*If everybody in our meetings started participating by sharing or exhorting, the meetings would become so horrendously long, and they'd last all day!* I have often suspected that we will become totally distracted by the sheer potential length of these new meetings when discussing this whole body-interaction thing. But, no one is saying that longer meetings are innately better, unless the length of the meeting helps create the synergism needed for the full mutual edification of everyone. The length of meetings is like a basketball game. If you and I are playing one-on-one on a half-court, that game will not likely go as long as complete teams in full-court press. More players, longer game.

So, when you add more players to the roster, with more people bringing songs, words, prophecies, drama, art, testimonies, and a myriad of responses, the meeting will naturally become longer. Again, more players, longer game. But is that all bad?

In the average church gathering, the players are usually the worship leader or worship team, and the speaker. Maybe some small parts have been set aside to be played out by someone giving the announcements or a special musical number or offertory—but not much more than that. In the rare case someone is actually allowed to preach the all-hallowed sermon, it is when someone gets suddenly ill, or the guest speaker has car trouble and misses the meeting.

Again, it is more than the length of the meeting. It is more about taking a long hard look at what we are doing to *"equip the saints for the work of ministry"* (Eph. 4:12a). If people look only to a pastor or professional leader, or even just a select "anointed" few, then there could be something wrong with this picture.

What does it mean to create an environment where others are drawn out, and called out to clear intentional ministry? What does it mean for you to relinquish some of your moment-by-moment control over every facet of the meeting? What does it mean to use your platform to create a "boot camp" for others to participate and learn?

When you first begin to let the ministry of your fellowship go and release more and more of it to others, you will go through a lot of changes and insecurities. At the same time, this could be the first step for many to find some edifying fulfillment in their own risk-taking and participation in ministry.

It starts by committing yourself to release the Body to talk, to sing, to prophesy, to share in the meetings. Try to find meetings where this can happen on a regular basis. If you don't have any such gatherings, create some. The size of the meeting has some bearing on how many can effectively and fruitfully share. So, if necessary, create some new kind of meeting for the purpose of releasing the Body to be the Body. But eventually this "Body life" must be allowed to creep into everything we do as the Church, by beginning to see yourself as a leader who leads through others, as well as one who brings his or her gift to the mix.

God has called us to lead, to equip, to give oversight. Sometimes this is best done by simply getting out of the way, and actually seeing whether or not our equipping ministry is doing just that—equipping!

Begin by praying for and encouraging those you influence to feel free to open up in your meetings with more and more "participation." Take personal responsibility and get them ready to participate. Teach them to come to those meetings with ample preparation of their hearts. Teach them to seek the Lord prior to meetings in such a way that they will feel motivated to come with gifts to freely give to others in the meeting. And as they begin to participate, give them more and more time to express what they bring to the meetings. Even put questions in front of them on a weekly basis so that they can begin to think proactively about the gathering during the week.

What can you bring to the meeting?

1) Can you bring a song?

2) Can you bring a report?

3) Can you bring a prophecy?

4) Can you bring an encouragement?

5) Can you bring a dance?

6) Can you bring a lesson?

7) Can you bring a poem?

8) Can you bring a skit?

When we see that the ministry of the church is not to be centered on just one person or ministry, but on a team, we confront the fallout of the "spectator spirit" of 21st-century Christianity that has produced some of our greatest problems.

It seems that one of the primary reasons for people becoming disgruntled, or even worse, bored, is because they feel "spiritually unemployed." They are not experiencing personal, ongoing fulfillment in their own mission and call. Every Christian has been given a calling and a ministry. They were known by God before the creation of the world, and called with a purpose. The frustration of not being equipped or given permission to fulfill what we have been created for, is causing many of the conflicts, battles, and church splits that happen these days.

I heard about a survey that asked Christians if they even knew what their gifting(s) were. Although 71 percent said they had heard about spiritual gifts, only 22 percent of the total believed that they could identify a spiritual gift they possessed, and 12 percent claimed they did not have a spiritual gift. This is horrific, but I do believe that freedom is coming. There is a new breed of leader rising up who will fulfill the mandate of true New Testament protocol to equip people, and allow them to do the ministry. This will come in many forms, but it will come. It has to.

SUCCESS MEANS EQUIPPING

A New Testament church leader is successful only if he or she is raising up others who can do what they do. A true leader is successful only to the degree that he or she is reproducing himself or herself. Now, for those who wonder about how this will grow their church, trust me, you'll have church growth! But it will not be just growing wide or big, but deep and strong.

Imagine church as not just another meeting held at a meeting place, with limited gift exposure through one or few gifts; instead, visualize a "fully-equipped" and "highly activated" group of believers living in virtual reality. Imagine church life returning to the concept of "share and tell," rather than "just come and get!"

Imagine a new breed of leaders actually becoming more excited about the daily and weekly Holy Spirit encounters of the people in the Body, rather than the numeric success of the weekend gatherings. One of my ministry mottos has always been that "the meeting place is the mentoring place for the market place."

Over the years I have personally seen a direct correlation between how a person is allowed to participate in a public meeting, and that individual's zeal and confidence in ministry outside the gathered church setting. If we can make room for people to share, to give a word of knowledge, a word of exhortation or comfort, even preach and teach in public meetings, we are indirectly helping them find their mission and their bearings for ministry outside the gathered church. If they can learn in an atmosphere of affirmation and safety within the church meeting, they can grow to minister in the hostile environment outside.

THE INTERRUPTING GOD

Of course, these kinds of open meetings are different than the average preplanned, scripted, and rehearsed one-way 45-minute lectures we are used to. They can feel chaotic, even out of order. The fact is, God seems to like them and has been doing this kind of divine interruption of our predictable meetings for centuries.

Frank Bartleman chronicled the heavy burden to keep the meetings open in the early days of the Azusa Street Revival as he notes:

> Those were Holy Spirit meetings, led of the Lord...
>
> When we first reached the meeting, we avoided human contact and greeting as much as possible. We wanted to meet God first.

No subjects or sermons were announced ahead of time, and no special speakers. No one knew what might be coming, what God would do. We all wanted to hear from God, through whomever He might speak.

The meetings started themselves, spontaneously, in testimony, praise and worship. We did not have to get one cue from some leader, yet we were free from lawlessness. Someone would finally get up, anointed for the message. All seemed to recognize this and gave way. It might be a child, a woman, or a man. No one wished to show himself. We only thought of obeying God. In fact, there was an atmosphere of God there that forbade anyone but a fool from attempting to put himself forward without the real anointing, and such did not last long. The Spirit ran the meeting from start to finish. There was no program, and hardly a chance for even necessary announcements. There was neither pulpit, nor organ, nor choir.

God came so wonderfully near us that the very atmosphere of heaven seemed to surround us. Such a divine "weight of glory" was upon us that we could only fall on our faces.

We had the greatest struggle with strange preachers who wanted to preach. Of all people, they seemed to have the least sense and did not know enough to keep still before Him. They liked to hear themselves. But many a preacher died to self in these meetings. The breath would be taken from them. Their minds would wander, their brains would reel. Things would turn black before their eyes. They could not go on. I never saw one get by with it in those days. They were up against God. He wound them up in short order. They were carried out dead, spiritually speaking. They generally bit the dust in humility.[1]

FUTURE LEADERS

As the Body gets freed up to "obey" the promptings of the Spirit, even in the main meeting, another thing happens. When we give permission to become a "ministering missional church," and not just a place for the applauding fans of the star minister, even the selection process for future leadership shifts. Every time we gather, we open our eyes. We get another opportunity to see "future leaders" in action. Church becomes the proverbial "farm league" where the coaches discover the next roster of players, the next batch of leaders.

As the conferences of today have replaced seminaries as the primary place of equipping for the future leaders of the Church, we must recapture the biblical pattern of leader-disciple, mentor-student, and coach-player. Life does more to prepare us for ministry than isolated institutions, ministry schools, or seminars. While many still cringe at the word "discipleship" because of some excesses in the past, this word must be recaptured.

Some might think I am advocating that pastors suddenly resign their churches and ministries, and go sell cars or insurance for a living. Not at all! I believe that leaders who are proactive and releasing have their best days in front of them—their finest hour. I know personally that I want to leave behind the legacy of an army of alive, activated, well-equipped disciples, who have both heart and confidence in ministry, rather than just leaving behind a stack of old teaching tapes that remind people of what a hardworking pastor I was. What about you?

ENDNOTE

1. Frank Bartleman, *Azusa Street* (New Kensington, PA: Whitaker House, 1982), 58-61,75,99.

Chapter Eight

GROUPS OF TENS, GROUPS OF FIFTIES, AND GROUPS OF HUNDREDS

WHEN the "saints movement" begins and the believers become fully acclimated to participating and not just observing, you will find yourself facing all of those old forms and models that have shut down and silenced God's people. What a release that is. Experimenting with new forms or models for doing church differently in the third millennium has unforeseen possibilities—not only for how we meet, but also for when and where and in what size these meetings take place for the optimum release of God's people.

As early as the mid-1970s, I was personally processing, at least in my mind, this whole idea of doing church differently. At the time I was reading books like *The Problem of Wineskins* by Howard Snyder, and listening to guys who were adamant that the classic small group of a dozen believers meeting in homes around a meal was the backbone of New Testament Church life, and needed to be restored to church life today.

Watchman Nee, in his classic, *The Normal Christian Church Life*, notes that there were at least two different kinds of meetings that were fundamental to New Testament Christians. He called them "church meetings" and "apostolic meetings." The first was the meeting of the "church" for itself, and the second was a meeting for the "work" of the church, or the mission or the apostolic vision of the church.[1]

In the first of these meetings, the "church" meetings, everyone contributes for the purpose of mutual edification. In the latter, the "apostolic" meetings, leaders teach and equip, releasing the character of the work of the church in a permissional and missional-sending dynamic. In the "church" meetings, "each one has a psalm, a teaching, a tongue, a revelation, an interpretation," as mentioned in I Corinthians 14:26. Here the case was not so much individuals leading and others listening, but rather, each contributing and sharing what they brought to the meeting. Even though, in most cases, only a few of those present actually contributed in any given meeting, all could have. A few were actual contributors, but all were potential contributors.

I would like to go a little farther than Nee and consider the possibility of several different sizes, or different kinds of meetings. Like most Christians of my generation, I was fed a pretty steady diet of three meetings a week—the Sunday morning worship service, the Sunday evening evangelistic service, and the Wednesday night prayer meeting. We had three meetings (at least we met three different times during a week). The problem was, they all were basically the same meeting, just at a different hour and with different amounts of people gathered.

All the meetings were usually held in the same room or building. We worshiped, gave announcements, offered special numbers, and listened to a sermon or Bible study, usually prepared by the pastor. The only thing that differed was the attendance. Only a "remnant," as it was described (a fancy biblical term used to label a small group), showed up for the midweek prayer meeting, and sometimes the pastor moved a preaching stand or music stand off the raised platform and put it down at floor level with everyone else. And of course, this was done so he could be more intimate with the remnant.

I even recall a person's spirituality was based upon which meeting he or she attended. Those who attended the Sunday morning meeting loved the church; those who attended the Sunday evening meeting loved the pastor; and those who attended the Wednesday evening prayer meeting loved the Lord. And man, if you came to all three—whew! You were the next pastor!

DIFFERENT SIZE, DIFFERENT OUTCOMES

It is not that we just need more than one meeting. In fact, it doesn't matter how many meetings you have in a week or a month. What is important is to see the potential of different sizes of meetings that create different atmospheres or venues, and thus produce different outcomes or results.

When you begin to adjust your schedules to meet in more definitive and intentional gatherings around different sizes, you will experience a fresh new wealth and health in being together. Smaller groups can gather in homes for meals, the breaking of bread and fellowship, growing in intimacy and nurture through mutual accountability. Medium-sized groups can gather where all the saints are free to take part in the meeting. And larger meetings can come together where the celebration level or scope of "vision casting" is significantly different than the smaller gatherings.

The potential of three or more different gatherings, three or more different expressions, three or more different ways of meeting, opens things to an even greater potential for any given area, community, city, or region.

The Old Testament seems to carry with it a breakdown of different-sized groups which, when seen in terms of group dynamics, can give us a very effective grid. Conducting meetings with different-sized groups, participating in different flows, and looking for different purposes involve more than just a quest for variety. It is as old as Exodus. Some have even called this the Jethro II Principle, as it refers to the counsel given by Jethro to Moses, his son-in-law, in order to help facilitate the gathering of Israel in different-sized groupings for maximum administration and care.

In Exodus 18:21, Jethro gives counsel to Moses to administrate the people of God in groups of tens, groups of fifties, groups of hundreds, and groups of thousands.

I must give the credit for this thinking about these different kinds, sizes, or configurations of meetings, to a very innovative leader I met in the early days of my journey with the Foursquare denomination. His name is Don Pickerill. He was sharing these principles of how to meet in these numerically defined groups as far back as the 1970s.

At the time, his entire fellowship was experimenting with them on an ongoing basis. During that era, many were beginning to experiment with different variations of these different-size groups, teaching that each size group provided a different way of being together, and a different setting for learning and doing things.

Pickerill taught about these various meetings and their individual dynamics by using creative word studies of each size. By meeting in these groups of tens, fifties, and hundreds, and by experiencing how they felt, how they flowed, and how each size-group carried a different focus, we would actually conduct meetings differently, and thus church differently. When we started meeting in these different-size groups, we found each to have an intrinsic dynamic. Each size encourages a different way of meeting—not just in terms of location, or room arrangement or seating, but also with unique components for each meeting size, and each group meeting the different needs of those who attend.

THE ESER OR GROUPS OF TENS

The word *eser* is the Hebrew word for the number ten, which represents the smallest division into which Moses put the people of God for the purpose of wise administration. *This is the group where everyone talks.*

These smaller groups are home-based, intergenerational meetings, where we share our lives on a regular basis, make our needs known to each other, and bear each other's burdens. This dynamic is experienced through a weekly meeting in our homes around the joy of a shared common meal and the restored richness of the Lord's Supper (see Acts 2:46).

These groups are not cell groups, or even home groups; they are real churches—complete and autonomous churches. They have leaders; they often receive offerings for missions, the poor, and needy. They evangelize the lost, baptize the converts, dedicate the babies, marry the wed and bury the dead, and obviously celebrate the sacrament of communion. These smaller groups are not just extensions of the "mother ship" local community church that has a central campus around which all life swirls. They are the Church.

This is church at its heart. Apart from the intimacy of lovers, there are few human actions that bind people to one another more closely than what the Romans called a *convivium*, their word for a banquet that literally means "living together."

We drop our defenses, feel grateful to be with our friends around the meal; we argue and discuss and quarrel and tease and laugh. Here, children watch their parents and learn about living. From the marriage feast of Cana to the Last Supper to His post-resurrection breakfast on the shore of the lake, Jesus loved to eat and drink with His friends. He used the imagery of the banquet for the Eucharist in which He leaves us His abiding presence. Jesus Himself was even known as someone who came "eating and drinking" (see Matt. 11:19).

In George Herbert's words: "You must sit down, says love, and taste my meat. So I did sit and eat." We simply "find Christ in the meal," making room for His meal, His Supper.

Shared meals construct and sustain human relationships. Inviting someone to share a meal powerfully symbolizes solidarity. Indeed, the word "companionship" comes from the Latin *cum* + *panis*, meaning, "breading together." Meals are social realities of great importance. Because meals express the very texture of human associations, they often exhibit social boundaries that divide human communities. We make decisions about not only what we will eat but with whom we will eat. Patterns of table sharing reveal a great deal about the way of life, the norms and commitments, of a particular community.

Within the Gospels, Jesus' meal patterns received special attention. Many of His critics observed, "This fellow welcomes sinners and eats with them" (see Luke 15:1-2; Mark 2:15-17; Matt. 11:19). They were shocked and appalled that Jesus welcomed everyone to His table. His behavior indicated acceptance and friendship with those who had been judged unfit for table fellowship—the tax collector, the Gentile, the prostitute. His open invitation "manifested the radically inclusive nature of his kingdom, a kingdom that cuts across the barriers we erect between insiders and outsiders, the saved and the damned, the elect and the outcast, barriers often most rigidly enforced at the table."[2]

PREPARING FOR A MEAL

This smaller group is summarized in two words: *eating* and *blessing*. Both activities are designed to "spur one another to love and good deeds." Both of these prophetic acts are designed to "strengthen, edify, encourage" fellow believers.

Eating the Lord's Supper, they broke bread in their homes and ate together with gladness (implies "exuberant joy") and sincerity (implies an "uncluttered simplicity") of heart (see Acts 2:46). Church takes place around the dinner table. The meal is the time to talk about what God is doing in our lives. It's the time to remember Jesus (see 1 Cor. 11:24).

- Tell how He blessed you in the last week.
- Tell what you are learning from His Word.
- Tell how He used a brother or sister to encourage you.
- Tell about God sightings.

- Tell Holy Ghost stories.
- Forget none of His benefits (see Ps. 103:1-2).

Bless one another during the meal. Speak blessings to one another, over, and through, and in the meal; blessings about our God-given identity (who we are); and blessings about our destiny (what God has made us to do). Toast one another, share how we see Jesus in each other, and strengthen one another through the meal.

- Friends to friends.
- Husbands to wives.
- Wives to husbands.
- Parents to children.
- Every believer to every other believer.
- Use passages of Scripture (see Col. 3:16).
- Use prayer.
- Use song (see Eph. 5:19).
- Use prophecy (see 1 Cor. 14:3).
- Use the laying on of hands.
- All at the direction of the Spirit.

The goal of a New Testament Church meeting is the building up of one another. That is the main reason we gather—not worship, not evangelism, and not teaching. The main reason the Church gathers is for the mutual edification of one another.

When today's gathered believer is asked why we gather, he usually responds with one of top four answers: *worship, evangelism, fellowship,* and *teaching*.

When God's people gather, there will be worship. Teaching will happen more likely in the moment, but it will happen. And even evangelism can take place, even though it comes best in the marketplace of life.

And of course, fellowship will happen because it is closest to the main purpose of the gathered Church. The point is, the Acts of the Apostles and Church history confirm that the main reason for the Church gathered is simply, plainly, and clearly for the expressed purpose of the mutual face-to-face building up of one another that occurs.

Consequently, only two activities are necessary to begin an *eser*— eating and blessing. Other things may flow out of these acts of *eating* and *blessing*, but this is the starting place.

As one brother said, "I'm so drawn to the idea of the table being a central part of life together as believers. It's natural; it gives a way to share our lives in a common, informal manner."

The worship of an early Christian house church was centered on the dinner table. They didn't sit facing forward as we think of people sitting in a church building today. But rather they were at someone's table, and the center of their activity was the fellowship meal or the communal meal.

The term *communion* actually comes from this experience of the dining fellowship. We need to remember that dining is one of the hallmarks of early Christian practice almost from the very beginning. All the Gospel traditions tend to portray Jesus at a meal as a very important part of His activity. Paul's confrontation with Peter at Antioch was over dining, and when we look at the context of the letters, especially First Corinthians, the role of dining in fellowship was central to all their religious understanding and practices.

As people around the meal start blessing each other while they are *eating*, even the new ones begin to catch this principle of *blessing*. They learn to listen to the Lord, and to give their blessings to others to strengthen and encourage each other.

MEALOLOGY: THE STUDY OF THE FULL MEAL

"Supper" is generally understood to refer to a full meal—enough food to satisfy the appetite. A portion of food that is less than a meal is typically thought to be a snack.

Considering the way most churches observe the Lord's Supper (with a sip of juice and a cracker remnant), why is it called a "supper"? Would it not be better to name it what it honestly has become? To many believers, the Lord's Supper is not a "supper" at all. It is the "Lord's Appetizer" or perhaps the "Lord's Hors D'oeuvres"! Did our Lord really intend to launch a memorial snack?

The Lord's Supper originated at the "last supper" (see Luke 22:7-38), which itself was a Passover feast. Have you ever looked up the word *feast* in the dictionary? A feast is an elaborate meal, a banquet, associated with abundant heaps of food. So it was with the Passover feast.

Luke wrote that at the last "supper" (see Luke 22:20), Jesus took the cup and said that it was "the new covenant in My blood, which is shed for you." The Greek word Luke used for "supper" is from the root noun *deipnon*. As you might expect, it means "dinner, supper, the main meal toward evening." It can also mean "formal dinner, banquet." This same word is used in Luke 14:15-24, where the NIV renders it a "great banquet" (see Luke 14:16).

Notice that when Jesus passed the cup around after the supper (see Luke 22:20), He had already taken the bread and said, "This is My body and will be given up for you" while the supper was in progress (see Luke 22:19; Matt. 26:26, Mark 14:22). The point to be observed is that the newly initiated Lord's Supper occurred in the midst of a full banquet, a full meal.

The Passover meal was transformed into something new—the Lord's meal. Would the twelve disciples have deduced from this that the Lord's Supper was somehow no longer to be a true meal?

In most study-Bibles, the topic heading for First Corinthians 11:17-34 is "The Lord's Supper" (or something similar). Though the Corinthians were officially meeting together to observe the Lord's Supper, they were abusing it so badly that Paul said it had ceased being the "Lord's" Supper (see 1 Cor. 11:20) and had instead become their "own" supper (see 1 Cor. 11:21 NAS). What blunders had they committed to create such a situation?

First, divisions existed among them (see 1 Cor. 11:18). Second, each of them went ahead and ate the Lord's Supper without waiting for the others (see 1 Cor. 11:21). The result? Those who arrived late went hungry and some of the earliest arrivals were already drunk (see 1 Cor. 11:21). Third, they failed to recognize the body of the Lord in the supper (see 1 Cor. 11:29).

So what was Paul's inspired solution to the Corinthian mess? Did he tell them to get rid of the meal?

The answer was that *"when you come together to eat, wait for one another"* (1 Cor. 11:33). As for those who were so famished that they were tempted to eat all the food ahead of time, Paul wrote, *"If anyone is hungry, let him eat at home"* (see 1 Cor. 11:34a).

Nowhere does Paul tell them to cease holding the Lord's Supper or reduce it to a snack-style memorial. What a violation of the theology behind the Lord's Supper.

One final (and important) word needs to be said about the form of the Lord's Supper. Within the full meal there still will be the bread and the cup. First Corinthians 10:16-17 mentions "the" cup and "the" loaf, stating, *"we, though many, are one bread and one body; for we all partake of that one bread."* It is important that we use one cup (or vessel) and one loaf in our Lord's Supper. The one cup and one loaf not only symbolize our unity as one body, but even create unity!

Again, why does the Church gather? Acts 20:7 says, *"On the first day of the week, when the disciples came together to break bread...."* The phrase "to break bread" is, in Greek, a "telic" infinitive, denoting a goal or purpose. Why did the Church come together on the first day of the week? In order to observe the Lord's Supper (see also 1 Cor. 11:33).

It seems the primary objective for the weekly gathering of the saints is to break bread. This allows God's people to enjoy fellowship, to mutually encourage and exhort each other, to share prayer requests, to tell what God is doing in their lives, to stimulate one another to love and good deeds, to be reminded of Jesus' sacrifice on the cross, to remind Jesus of His promise to return, and to be made into one body through the one loaf. This truth bears repeating.

The primary activity that a church is to engage in during their meeting or gathering is the eating of the Lord's Supper as a full meal. All else is secondary to this and is therefore optional. This means that we do not assemble weekly to hold a worship service, nor to hear preaching, nor to have a praise meeting, nor for an evangelistic out-reach, nor for any other reason.[3]

In fact, evangelism happens around an open table. In the Lord's Supper, the followers of Jesus Christ are called to practice eating as He ate, to be a people of gratitude and generosity, of openness and accept-ance. They are summoned to be a community where amazingly diverse people allow themselves to be formed by one Lord into one body around a common table. When our table is less than the fullness of Christ's invitation, we eat and drink judgment (see 1 Cor. 11:29).[4]

CONCLUSION #1

The local church does not *do* small groups; the local church is a small group where everyone participates.

THE MISSIM OR GROUPS OF FIFTIES

The Hebrew word *missim* is the number 50, again taken directly from Exodus 18:21, and is the second administrative grouping of the people of God. *This is the group where everyone worships*. It possibly represents one of the best ways, if understood geographically, to gather several smaller groups together in a given area for the effective expression of cooperation and participation. These groups are not meant to replace the whole body, but rather make possible a type of meeting in which all ages, including children, can participate.

The central principle behind this meeting seems to be best defined as "a spirit of prophecy" (see Rev. 19:10). Even before the advent of the Holy Spirit, when prophecy rested on a choice few, Moses yearned and longed for the coming day of maturity when all God's people would become ministers and speak on God's behalf. *"Oh, that all the Lord's people were prophets and that the Lord would put His Spirit upon them!"* (Num. 11:29b).

- This meeting is based upon the full priesthood of all believers with mutual edification and mutual up-building for the purpose of personal strengthening, similar to the model that we find in First Corinthians 14:26.

- This meeting is centered on interactive and creative worship through prayers, songs, dance, mime, drama, art, exhortation, etc. (see Eph. 5:19).

- In this meeting, the children have a "song." These meetings do not need to be led by a set worship team of musicians or singers.

NOTE: When we say "worship," please keep in mind that we are not referring to just songs with lyrics and music. Unless worship becomes more than the music that fills our meetings, only the musicians or composers or singers will be released. What about the artists, the poets, the mimes, the stand-up comics, the actors, or even the chefs and the inventors?

- In this meeting, each one could have an appropriate "word" to share, and the reading of the Scripture and the sharing of truth could be both planned and/or spontaneous.

- In this meeting, God can and will speak through many individuals. These expressions of "revelation" can be what the Spirit is saying to the group, or even what the Spirit is saying through one individual to another through edification and encouragement.

This expression can be done by gathering several smaller house churches or simple churches into a larger setting, a bigger home, a large backyard, park, beach, and celebrating a child-like party with believers who already enjoy gathering weekly or monthly in their homes, or more often when the weather is good.

THE MEA OR GROUPS OF HUNDREDS

Mea or the word for a number of hundreds in Hebrew, once again shows the prudent administrative potential available as a group reaches this size. This is a gathering with a larger expression than that of tens or fifties. *This is the group where everyone listens and learns.*

This is where group dynamics must shift. There is a principle that states that if everyone in a group cannot potentially do what a single member does, the group dynamic changes. A larger group meeting requires a different set of dynamics to make that meeting the most meaningful.

In these larger meetings, the emphasis is on the direction of church in the region or the network of churches in the region (see Acts 13:15-41; 1 Tim. 4:13). In these larger gatherings, the corporate, prophetic worship celebration and the gifting of the apostolic and prophetic leaders of the regional apostolic team are needed to cast the vision for the benefit and the equipping of the whole group.

These larger meetings are not usually led by a single leader, but by regional teams, generally formed by the coalescing of the local fivefold ministries in the region.

Apostolic/prophetic leaders, as hinted in First Corinthians 12:28 and Ephesians 2:20 tend to be very successful in linking those Christians within a geographic region, a distinct locale, or a specific county.

DYNAMIC AND DIFFERENT

Each meeting then, has its own optimum style and works to release a certain size-directed effect or dynamic. Experimenting with these meetings or hybrids, combinations, or mixtures of these meetings really does catch the heart of God for doing church differently.

The ten-size group meeting best allows for the church to keep its foundation relational and covenantal. A fifty-size group meeting best allows for a group-centered emphasis. And a hundred-size group meeting best allows for a vision-centered emphasis.

Actually, these meetings are more about how they each feel, and how that dynamic or feel changes as numbers go up or down. You literally have to feel the group, and sense how the dynamic has shifted rather than concentrate on a fixed ratio or size. The small group is about home, about fellowship, about the dynamic of family. It feels like the family where everyone matters, and everyone is a part.

Any time it feels bigger than that (sense of family), it automatically shifts into more of a gift-centered dynamic where the multiple imput of others must be facilitated as the size grows. Many times the shift is so automatic, it moves on its own to a Q & A format, and can no longer linger in the home-style, face-to-face fellowship that a family enjoys around a meal.

And as gatherings continue to grow in size, it requires more and more of a strategic adjustment as you move away from the individual focus of the small group, past the gift focus of the medium-size group, to more of an apostolic team approach in facilitating the larger gathering, the event, the conference, that is more vision focused. We'll talk more about the effect of the larger meeting in Chapter Sixteen, "Church: Simple and Regional."

Different-size meetings, different venues, and different dynamics all play a part in "doing" church differently in this third millennium.

ENDNOTES

1. Watchman Nee, *The Normal Christian Church Life* (Anaheim, CA: Living Stream Ministry, 1980), 172.

2. W.H. Willimon, *The Service of God: How Worship and Ethics Are Related* (Nashville, TN: Abingdon, 1983), 133.

3. John White. *Simple Church* www.housechurchchronicles. typepad.com/.

4. Darrell L. Gruder, *Missional Community: A Vision for the Sending of the Church in North America* (Grand Rapids, MI: Eerdmans), 164-165.

Chapter Nine

WHAT'S REALLY SACRED?

IT really is true that you never know how sacred something is until you touch it, try to move it, or God forbid, actually stop it or kill it. Just try to worship past the sacred noon hour, and watch everyone check their watches and clear their throats. Just try to have the pastor sit down to make room for others to actually participate in the meeting, and watch as everyone gets fidgety. Just start releasing the uneducated, the untrained, the unordained, or even just the young to serve communion, to bring direction, or actually lead a meeting, and get ready for the e-mails. Just try to have church on any other day than Sunday. Just try to have church in any other place other than the regular, stained-glass, womb church building.

Just start encouraging people to have church in their homes or at work or any other place. Start encouraging church to be practiced in any other way than we have done for the last 200-plus years in this country, and Pastor, you'd better be ready for a fight. Or, heaven forbid, just cancel church some Sunday and do something else, and you might as well look for some new kind of work.

TOUCHING THE "SACRED"

Just how sacred are these things? Again, just try to touch them or change them or stop them, and you'll probably find out. Okay, I know what you are thinking. You're thinking this preacher's kid needs deliverance. He is simply mad at the church, needs inner healing, or should be attending the newest Twelve-Step Program for Preacher's

Kids Anonymous! But, believe it or not, I really do love the Body of Christ, and I am madly in love with the Head of the Church, and yes, I actually love gathering with God's people. What I am frustrated with are the traditions and constrictions that limit the overall possibility of the Church being the Church. I am asking those hard questions of who is church for? Why do we meet when we meet? Why do we meet where we meet? And, why do we do certain things when we do meet?

It is in these matters that I still end up with many more open-ended questions than simple, neatly tied-up, packaged answers.

I have observed that by comparison to most other themes, the New Testament is conspicuously silent about what is to happen when we meet, or what it is to look like, or why it is that we consider so important the things we do. As frightening as it may appear, I believe that the Father left far more of this stuff up to us than we have been willing to take responsibility for. We all know that so many of the things we deem important or even sacred, don't even show up in the guide book (the Bible)—Sunday school, youth group, nursery, junior choir. And what about buildings and boards, or even weekly sermons?

It seems clear that God knows that our styles, culture, societal trends, likes and dislikes, or even just personal tastes and disdains will ultimately play far more of a role in dictating and determining how we do this thing called "church" than we can even imagine. So really, when it comes to touching these "sacred things," before we "have a cow" (you know what I mean—a sacred one!), let's at least be willing to ask the questions.

Exactly who are these things sacred to, or for? Are they sacred to my old pastor, my Bible college professor, Aunt Mildred, Christians in the Midwest, or me? And don't be so bold as to answer for God. Instead, let's own our own personal biases, our own private bents, and take responsibility for the choices we make. The Father seems very clear in His Word on what He likes and dislikes, and also on the freedoms He has given us. So, first of all, let's not try to preach from silence, because the Bible does not teach that the junior choir should sing first, followed by the offering, and then the adult choir. And, let's at least give God a break before we say, "Wow, don't touch that, that is sacred!" And admit, that at best (or worst), it is sacred or important to us, and we are not to be speaking for God.

THE LAST HOLDOUT

In my observations, one of the last "holdouts" that God is dealing with as He changes the shape and forms of today's Church is the sermon. It's the "Alamo." It's "Custer's Last Stand," or even worse, the "Ark of Sacredness." When it comes to the things we are willing to adjust, alter, or change, the sacred sermon, the holy homily, is the last to go. Given the reality that the average pastor is judged, praised, crucified, or deified for his weekend oratory, it is no wonder that he spends most of his waking hours (and sometimes not-so-waking hours) preparing, polishing, and practicing this Protestant performance ethic.

Unfortunately, it is also the thing that can represent so much of a pastor's personal identity, the part he plays in the whole scheme of the church. Today's sermon stands as the centerpiece of the average evangelical gathering. And he is called "pastor" in today's ecclesiastical system, based upon the perception of his peers, his colleagues, and even his constituents because of his ability or lack thereof to "preach" or "teach" or "sermonize." Thus, the common interpretation of that famous list of gifts in Ephesians 4 of apostles, prophets, evangelists, and pastor-teachers, could just as well read, "apostles, prophets, evangelists, and sermonizers." Yet the word "sermon" does not even appear in Scripture.

We can give up the worship leading to others (if they can sing). We can give up the prayers, the prophecies, and even the "sacred" announcements. Maybe even the "all-sacred" offering can be led or officiated by someone else. Maybe, just maybe (depending on your liturgical bent), even the administering of communion or the Lord's

Supper can be given to another (as long as he is a qualified elder and the husband of "one" wife). But no one, under any circumstances, simply no way (unless we are on vacation when the proverbial itinerant guest speaker comes in, or some missionary on furlough) is someone going to take our sermon away. Well, yes...maybe the Holy Spirit, but that is only a time or two in a year...but absolutely no one else.

Of course, there is a place, and a strong biblical place, for proclamation and teaching, a deliberate call for the equipping of the saints, and for living in truth. It's how we do it that has become all too traditionalized and ritualized. What is behind the fact that pastors are the only ones who can consistently preach or teach? And not just the content of the sermon, but the mode, the way, the means through which the message is given, need to be thought through. If we know that our target audience has changed and evolved, and demand more, there must be a shift. In addition, there really is no biblical support for the "talking head" model of "one man teaches all."

For God's sake, and the people's sake, let's reevaluate our delivery systems to give this truth that we carry and cherish, a better and a richer chance of finding root. Today's listener, in the classic lecture hall of biblical learning (regardless of how gifted the speaker is) needs help. If not, then listening is simply all that might be accomplished. And that will be left with something to be desired.

Assuming that your Powerpoint presentation, with the three-step alliteration, followed by the two forms of application through drama and song, and the fill-in handouts seems by comparison to the stock lecture, far more effective. And people seem to be hearing, and/or visualizing much better, thus more retention and more application. Surely, this is the best we can do—right? Or is it?

Or should we still wonder whether today's praise concerts and multimedia presentations are actually working. We may be creating a more contemporary listening environment—at least by comparison to the drone sermons in the poorly lit catacombs of the past; but are we really creating a better learning experience? The acoustics may be better, but what about the full application and what about the overall actual effect on today's listener?

It seems that even the most basic laws of teaching and learning are being ignored as we seem more concerned with winning the contest of the "best show in town" rather than maintaining an all-out commitment that the people we lead and love actually learn. John Milton Gregory's *The Seven Laws of Learning* are more critical to today's listening audience than ever.

1) Know thoroughly and familiarly the lesson you wish to teach...teach from a full mind and a clear understanding.

2) Gain and keep the attention and interest of the pupils upon the lesson. Do not try to teach without attention.

3) Use words understood in the same way by the pupils and yourself...language clear and vivid to both.

4) Begin with what is already well-known to the pupil upon the subject and with what he himself has experienced...and proceed to the new material by single, easy, and natural steps, letting the known explain the unknown.

5) Stimulate the pupil's own mind to action. Keep his thought as much as possible ahead of your expression, placing him in the attitude of the discoverer, an anticipator.

6) Require the pupil to reproduce in thought the lesson he is learning...thinking it out in its various phases and applications till he can express it in his own language.

7) Review, review, review, reproducing the old and deepening its impression with new thought, linking it with added meanings, finding new applications, correcting any false views, and completing the true.[1]

INFORMATION OR TRANSFORMATION?

I feel like the church, particularly when it comes to being the pur-veyor of truth, has fallen into the "cram for the exam" form of teach-ing rather than the peripatetic model of Jesus. In Christ's day, the raboni (teacher) daily walked and taught and shaped people, not through lectures and diatribes only, but through the learner's lan-guage that solicited a corresponding responsiveness to life lessons.

The missing ingredient today is not more high-tech communica-tion devices, but an atmosphere of community where learning actu-ally takes place. My experience is that we learn best in the context of an environment that incorporates both *accountability* and *responsibility*.

For example, you have just heard a great sermon on prayer—in fact, possibly the greatest sermon on prayer you have ever heard. It was even deftly illustrated by the synergy of the choir, the drama team, and the ten-foot visuals splashed against the wall. You turn to your neighbor and comment about the power of that sermon, and even on the way out of the sanctuary you press towards the "preach-er-line" to congratulate your pastor with a "high-five" for a job well done.

Now, have you really gotten the message? Or, are you just swept away by the MTV-style of presentation? What have you really learned? Will this great sermon fall into that category of another great lesson your creative communicator produced that makes you feel good about being a part of this particular fellowship?

Again, don't get me wrong. I know that preachers and preaching are necessary (see Rom. 10:14) to proclaim the Good News to the lost. I am asking some the bigger question: How do we really learn? Or, at least, how do we learn better? I am all for the enhancing of not only the learning environment, but also the progressive art of teaching or preaching.

I want to suggest that we need to push this idea of truly learning and being *transformed*, rather than just being *informed*, by looking at not only how we teach, but also what kind of environment we are creating.

INTENTIONAL COMMUNITY

Let's return to the great sermon on prayer. What if, when you turned to your friend to remark as to how good the message was, you also included this response: "Hey, you know, I don't want to file this one in the great-sermons-of-the-past category in my brain. I want to really get prayer this time. Would you be willing to meet with me and help me? Would you simply be willing to hold me accountable to being transformed by this truth, rather than just being informed about it? Could we meet weekly for coffee, continue to read the Scriptures and other books on prayer together, and press in to make this prayer thing a lifestyle?"

Now you tell me, which response has the possibility of producing the most actual growth in your life in the area of prayer? Is it the ten-week series by the pastor on the prayer of Jabez, or that weekly mutual mentoring of brotherhood and community? I know that brings up the question: How do we even begin to encourage and foster, or birth or initiate or motivate people to live in this kind of intentional community? I guess that is my point. It seems to me that the goal of the church, rather than just becoming a more prolific dispenser of facts and figures, is to be a connector of people.

Being connected, not just consuming, is what changes people. It is people walking through life together on the same journey. It is not independent believers passing each other in the foyers of the average Sunday school building at a typical meeting hour to hear another Top-Ten presentation of the latest topic on "Nightline" that really makes disciples and followers of Christ.

Wolfgang Simson in *Houses That Change The World* reminds us that when it comes to communication theory, the Western concept of teaching, where the teaching is usually an address—a professional monologue geared at students in an academic setting removed from real life, has been proven to be a most ineffective teaching tool.

STATIC VERSUS KINETIC

In the West, the style is often static. The classic classroom approach is where the teacher is indoctrinating the passive crowd, trying to put across his or her points. True to a Greek and Roman concept of scholasticism and intellectualism, the goal is handing down knowledge.

On the other hand, the Eastern teaching style is kinetic—the topic of discussion literally moves from person to person, and everyone is involved. After such deliberation, a consensus is built, a collective opinion emerges, and corporate action can follow where questions and interaction reign. Over the ages, this has proven to be the most effective in changing opinions and values and, therefore, in changing people. Even the Greek word that is often translated "preaching," is actually the New Testament word *dialogizomai*, which means, "You've got it" dialogue between people!

Scientists have warned us for years that we remember a meager 10 percent of what we read; 20 percent of what we hear; 30 percent of what we see; 50 percent of what we hear and see; 70 percent of what we say ourselves; 90 percent of what we do ourselves. Another study indicates that on average, lectures to a crowd of people result in very limited information retention. Within 20 minutes of hearing a message, people forget 40 percent of the content; they lose 60 percent within half a day of the message; and within one week the average listener can recall only 10 percent of what was said.[2]

Well then, you decide—what is the optimum form of learning? Is it the boring, pedantic, one-way lecture, or a teaching style that may include a short talk (not a typical sermon), some illustrations, parables and stories, and is accompanied by healthy interruptions of questions and answers?

Remember, this could also mean an entire change in the building, the meeting time, the way you set the chairs, and basically the whole format, as you create a new environment where people connect in order to learn. This community style of teaching is geared to help people become "doers of the Word" teaching them to not just hear, but to *obey*, to *do* everything Jesus taught us (see Matt. 28:20).

Many feel that this pattern of learning is what the early Church enjoyed best, as it was patterned after the synagogue as a house of study and open discussion (see Acts 2:42). However, when Gentiles brought their one-man-in-charge customs and lecterns, their meetings eventually became closed to real participation. Only authorized clergy taught others to guard against heresies.

What is it about the American church that people love to shuffle in and out of the church building on the weekend, remaining anonymous all week long? Could it be that the meetings feel so academic that we have inadvertently taught entire generations of Christians to prefer "sound bites" of information rather than making a lifelong commitment to the lengthy journey of the processing of truth as a learning community of friends?

Gene Edwards, in his lightning-rod book, *Beyond Radical*, passionately reminds us through his research on weekly sermons that rather than being a New Testament pattern or tool, they date back to Aristotle as he taught the subject of rhetoric (Greek: *retorik*...the art of the orator), and to John Chrysostom in Antioch Syria, circa A.D. 400. As one of the great orators of all time, John (John the Goldenmouth) left his obvious stamp of Aristotelian rhetorical/sermon skills on modern-day Christianity.[3]

First-century Christian preaching was more characterized by being extemporaneous, spontaneous, and urgent...and it belonged to the entire Body of believers, not to a special class of men trained in Aristotle's concepts of oration.

I know you are desperate, just like I am. I know that you take your task of leading and making disciples as seriously as any pastor or leader who lives with that unshakable call on his or her life. And I know you want to be more effective, just like I do, for the people who God has given us to influence.

A RADICAL CALL

I want to suggest that, in our true desperation, we stop putting all our energies into "technique Christianity." I want to suggest that even as the Western church model ups the pace, hikes the price, and adds the pressure to attract the multitudes to their great weekend services (and in some case, "shows" best describe the services), that we no longer tolerate this "idolatry of information" that allows people to leave one more meeting without being changed, and that we give ourselves to the thorough ongoing challenge of a radical call to a community that produces an atmosphere for transformation.

Let's create a context for learning where the saints are released to grow together, to interact together, to listen together, to respond together, and to teach together. Let's remember that this true learning, this true fellowship happens not from better lectures or more fine-tuned presentations, but from a way of being with each other which changes how we relate, listen, and learn. If you are boring people to death, even with your best, well-intentioned, well-tuned, and well-meant, three-part, sermonic lifestyle, then stop. Find new ways of communicating truth.

If your people are addicted to you and continue to rely on your professional wit and wisdom as their main form of grazing and gleaning needed principles to live by, at least inform them and let them experience, even in that sacred weekend meeting, more effective forms of grasping truth through questions and answers, open interaction, and feedback.

What a call the Church of today has! It is to be the beacon to preach good news, understanding that if they know the truth, it will set them free (see John 8:32). Let's take this assignment to heart and create places and forms that help people learn and not just listen.

ENDNOTES

1. John Milton Gregory, *The Seven Laws Of Learning* (Grand Rapids, MI: Baker Book House, 1986), 19-20.

2. Wolgang Simson, *Houses That Change The World* (Waynesboro, GA: Authentic, 2001), 85-86.

3. Gene Edwards, *Beyond Radical* (Sargent, GA: The Seedsowers, 1999), 26-27.

Section Four

THIRD-DAY TRANSITION

Chapter Ten

CHARACTER AND TRANSITION—
PART ONE

IT is so exciting to walk with God, especially through these days of obvious change. Prayers we have prayed are finding answers. Dreams and aspirations are coming alive in our midst. I have never known a time, in my entire walk with the Lord, when His presence has been so profound and tangible. His love, kindness, mercy, and generosity are everywhere, it seems.

To be able to express love for God in worship is a great honor. The love and affection of Jesus for His Bride is enormous. To be able to reciprocate that love to honor His personality and the way He works is a great blessing, one that we do not deserve. To be included by a God who is so inclusive is a great honor.

To know what the Lord is building and to be able to place ourselves in His path, so that we are not obstacles to the world of change but participants in His great endeavor—this is our prayer. It is to perceive the hand of God at work and not spoil it by being carnal.

We need His wisdom, grace, and truth to touch our church situation in this time of change. We must have revelation that provides impetus to the Spirit and a rationale for our thinking.

Transition has a character attached to it. Transition is not just about changes in structure, style, and strategy; it is about diversity into new prototypes as well as conformity into the image and nature of Jesus. There is a provocation of the Spirit on all levels within and around our lives. In transition, the war between the Holy Spirit and the flesh is intensified. We learn how to hunger and thirst after God in a disciplined and not purely spontaneous manner.

Transition is about being made uncomfortable by events, as well as being comforted by the Holy Spirit. Transition is about pain, difficulty, and suffering as well as about a new joy and peace in believing. It is about forsaking sin and abandoning oneself to the cause of God. It is about our sacrifice and His glory.

Whatever we have to give up is negligible compared to the majesty and greatness of His presence. Whatever we give of ourselves is returned back to us pressed down, shaken together, and running over. He gives Himself. The prize is still knowing Jesus in all His fullness.

Transition is also about warfare and perseverance; it's standing our ground and discovering Jesus as the Warrior King. It is about perceiving His majesty and supremacy in such a profound way that our life radically changes. We become real warriors, not just weekend soldiers.

The whole world of the Church is going through a transition whether we like it or not; whether we understand it or not; whether we are prepared for it or not. Jesus is coming whether we are ready or not! Heaven is pressing down upon us, bending us out of shape. We have not built a church capable of welcoming the manifest presence of God. We have built a church for our ministry, not His.

In transition, everything heats up. The flesh gets hotter under the collar because it is being burned up. Passion for Jesus increases. Excitement rises up in worship, and our prayer becomes more fervent. The temperature is rising. The Holy Spirit is infusing us with a new energy so that we can rise up out of the tiredness we feel. Transition *is* tiring. We need God's power to stand up under it. Transition is about laying down everything we are and taking up everything that He is. Transition is necessary upheaval.

It is the passing of one dimension and the release of another. In the difficulty of changing over, we console ourselves with the fact that we asked for all this! Remember all those prayers of "Lord, change us; do something new; pour out Your Spirit in a fresh way. Father, we don't want to be stuck in this place; we want to move on in the Spirit"? Remember those? If you prayed anything remotely like that...it's your fault!

After the prayer comes the frustration. This is the irritation, the aggravation that is sent by God to provoke us to more prayer. Frustration is the provocation of God to enforce change quickly. It will not leave us alone; it grips us. It makes us examine the old and explore the new. Frustration is the plank of wood that bridges the chasm between two dimensions. We know it is risky. We can go only one step at a time. However, we have found that it is more faith-destroying to stay where we are than to risk the adventure of change. Put your foot on the plank and let's go together.

NEW MODEL CHURCHES

There will be hundreds of different types of churches, all finding their place together in the Body of Christ. The next dimension will be taken up with a very strong Kingdom ethos. No single church will rise up with the whole revelation, anointing, or understanding of what God is doing.

No single church will be the prototype. In cities, towns, and rural areas we will find numerous types of church, each holding a piece of the jigsaw. It will only be when we bring the pieces together in a Kingdom setting that we will begin to demonstrate the Kingdom desire that sits closer to the heart of God.

Building church without a desire for the Kingdom puts a restraining order on it from Heaven in terms of how far the work can go. If we do not build with Kingdom in mind, then we build something that reflects our own ego. What we are constructing has its foundation in empire—a personal domain of the anointed man of God whose own anointing is greater than the church he has built because his people are passive observers of all that God is doing with him. How tedious it is to be part of a church where the anointed one is sold out to his own ministry.

In His mercy, the Lord has allowed us time to grow up and work these things through. Transition is about the destruction of empire and the refocus on Kingdom. It is better for us to fall on this rock and be broken and humbled before God than for it to fall upon us and crush all that we have built in the name of Jesus...but with an eye out for ourselves.

We must humble ourselves and put everything into His hands so that He can decide whether we are trustworthy. If God did not own the getting of our ministry, He will not own the having of it—not without making Himself unrighteous. If we cheated others, broke our word, trod on people, used and discarded people, or promoted ourselves to get where we are, we need to repent right quick! Make restoration where God leads you, because the shaking has already begun.

Other churches matter. Say it every day: "Other churches matter. The Kingdom is more important." Establish the Kingdom and build the Church, in that order. As you build the Church, build Kingdom into your people. Other churches matter. Pray for them; have a heart for their growth. Have a desire to participate in the development of the whole Body of Christ across the whole area.

It will not guarantee revival. However, the water level of the Kingdom will rise enough in our hearts to prevent us from building our own empire, however small. If we plan to be inclusive and work with others where we can, at least the Lord will not have to shake or dismantle our work later on.

We can build a net between churches and cities. Each church will represent a knot in that net, a place where certain lines meet and join together. When the net is strong enough to bear the weight of what God wants to do in Kingdom, we will see some action. God works according to man's preparation and placement. The early Church was in one place and of one accord when Pentecost came. Can our sense of preparation and placement be any less?

The Lord is sharpening the Church at this time. He is putting a cutting edge on what we are doing. He is raising up a prophetic Church, one that is led by every word out of His mouth. It is a Church led by the Spirit, not one necessarily with systems, zones, or management strategies. The ministry of the Church will reflect God's relaxed but disciplined approach. On the surface it looks chaotic, because God is not a manager; He is a facilitator. Underneath the action, though, there is a calm order that arises out of God's character and nature.

Many leaders are not restful people. They are activity-oriented, or organizationally productive. The basis of this order comes from within. However, it is the anointing to be at rest, calm, and peaceful before God and man. It is the capacity to step back into God in times of tension and trouble, to know His rest and peace.

The work of the Church is full of the tension of many differences in ministry, many dissimilar people, and many contrasting applications of gifting. The capacity for chaos is endless. A little organization around this is fine. We need enough strategy to keep things broadly moving in the right direction. But too much organization will stifle creativity, spontaneity, and initiative.

Organization may create order in the world of business, education, and research, but it does not create order in the Church. The Church is a supernatural body, one where the chain of command is less obvious. It is the goal of leadership to teach everyone how to hear God's voice and to be led by the Spirit. It is the goal of leadership to train, equip, empower, and release the saints into the work of the ministry. It is the goal of leadership to follow after God so closely themselves that they become a model, a pattern, and an example worth following. It is the goal of leadership to facilitate, through friendship and trust, a proper framework for accountability that is powerful and relational without being based on some armed forces structure.

It is the goal of leadership to produce whole, healthy Christians who can take initiative, be led by the Spirit, and cause the enemy endless trouble. However, if our structure and chain of command is too rigid, we make it easy for the enemy to stop us from being effective. Yet if the majority of our people are capable of releasing salvation, healing, and deliverance as well as leading a small group, then we have a church based on interdependence that is difficult to pin down for the count. If the enemy opposes one part, another part rises up.

When persecuted in one area, we rise up elsewhere; when attacked in one spot, we pop up somewhere else; when opposed in that part, we return to the first place and recommence.

In the Church, too much order removes the supernatural edge that truly confounds the devil. Too much order makes us predictable and very, very ordinary. If our people spend more time learning about order, structure, who to report to, how to make referrals, chains of command, and accountable organizational behavior, they will not develop the initiative, creativity, order, and spontaneity of the Holy Spirit. We will have a man-centered ministry, not a Spirit-led one.

I like organization. I believe in structure. However, I would love for more leaders to be restful, peaceful, facilitating, trusting, and calm individuals in God, so that they can operate these things properly.

If we want the approval of God, we will have to face the annoyance of the world. The new prototype of church will anger the world. They will preach at us in anger because we have dared to go back to our roots. They want us to be familiar, predictable, and toothless. Obviously, familiarity is good when it relates to the character of the Church—its kindness, goodness, love of people, mercy, and reliability. People should be able to count on the nature of the Church being one with the character of our Lord.

However, in many places the Church has become an institution of convenience. We give, but we have no voice. We can comfort, but we cannot challenge. We are seen but are not heard. Tolerance has been stretched to embrace sin—to cover it without dealing with it. We do not have the disapproval or enmity of the world; we have their derision and contempt.

There is a new prototype, the first in a series, of church emerging that will clash with the world and institutional Christianity. The Church will rediscover her radical edge, but not by playing with the world's toys and using them differently. Real radical behavior in church is grounded in the supernatural. It proceeds from the mouth of God; it emanates from simple obedience to His ways; it emerges out of Holy Spirit boldness to follow the plans of God with fervent faith. It is to be willing to look foolish in order to confound the world.

We all will be pioneers in this next move of God. His plans for our churches will mean profound changes to the structure, vision, personality, and effectiveness of our meetings, missions, training, and discipleship forums. We will see a radical change in leadership style and methodology.

When building a prototype church, all mistakes are public. One thing we should note here: Real pioneers do not criticize other pioneers because they know how hard it can be to build something new. Unfortunately, though, settlers usually make the most vicious of critics. They haven't done it themselves and have no intention of taking what they perceive to be insane risks. Their credo is that it is better to snipe from the sidelines and then borrow the new thing once it has been proved out. Some even argue that it is their "refining" comments that have played a valuable part in maturing the original concept.

I guess we will find out what the Lord thinks of this type of behavior on the day of judgment. Unhappily for some, they will probably reap from what they have sown a little earlier than they would like.

When we go through times of testing with our new prototype, we will have an audience of both well-wishers and critics who have no honor and less mercy. It is true that the design stages will be fraught with problems. Our raw material will be people. Some will be able to stand the strain and stress; others will be caught out by the sacrifice and hard work. In any case, no one likes to fail. However, it is not all about success or failure, but primarily about learning and growing. It is about pressing on through the disappointments. It is about believing in the vision God has given and learning how not to do something before it suddenly clicks into place.

The Lord does not measure success by results, but rather by the faithfulness we display toward Him and His vision. Pioneering is about faithfulness to the call God has given us. Yet many of us are faithful only to ourselves. This self-preservation will always separate the true pioneers from those who progress only at other people's expense.

Some prototype churches will have a broad base of ministry; others will have a narrow field of operation. Some will look after several people-groups; others may base their ministry around one type. I know churches that cater to such groups as youth, people on the drug scene, and people of a certain nationality or economic type. It is exciting to see the many flavors that exist in the wider Body of Christ.

True spiritual conformity is only about being made over in the image of the Lord Jesus Christ. Jesus came to put a face on God. "He who has seen Me has seen the Father" (John 14:9). We are here to put a face on Christ. By our character, we demonstrate His nature.

The operation of the Church in ministry must reveal all the creative diversity in the heart of God. The broad dimension of anointing in the Holy Spirit cannot be contained within a single church, network, or organization. We must love and appreciate different ministries and befriend one another to help, shape, and support the full work of the Kingdom through the Church.

SHARING PERSPECTIVE WITH THE HOLY SPIRIT

God is breaking us out of stereotypes and using prototype churches that are often prophetic. They have groundbreaking concepts and people who understand the process of turning potential into something actual. They can handle frustration because they know it is a critical part of growth. This growth cannot happen apart from a general dissatisfaction with the current state. This provokes us to move forward, to seek the face of God for a new initiative. This is how vision is redefined and where our calling is made clearer in our hearts and minds.

We often are provoked on two levels—first, by satisfaction, and second, by comparison. God fills our mouth with good things and we are blessed. Some things are working well and we rejoice. By contrast then, our blessed state in one area highlights a pressing need in another. By comparison, we are less happy and dissatisfied with this particular part of our life and ministry that needs attention. By contrast and comparison, our blessings highlight our needs. We enjoy the good, and we strive toward progression in the other areas. We simply want to transfer the blessing of God across every area of life and ministry.

To progress in the Lord through the tribulation of our current experience, we must learn to share perspective with the Holy Spirit. It is right for us to tell Him how we feel so that He can comfort us. However, comfort is not agreement.

There are times when God's words do not comfort—they sting! That is because we want God on our side. However, He has no side but His own! To be truly comforted, we must see our situation from God's angle. Comfort will come not by understanding God's perspective, but by adjusting to it. Real comfort comes through submission.

There is always more happening than we can see at surface level. Sharing perspective with the Holy Spirit will open up our situation on several levels, notably the conscious and the unconscious. That which is hidden has greater power of revelation than that which is obvious. It is the digging for truth that opens our heart to it, not merely picking it up off the ground. The things that are seen are temporal, but that which is hidden is eternal (see 2 Cor. 4:18). What is happening on a visible, conscious level is quite different from what is being revealed through the hidden, unconscious dimension. The Holy Spirit who searches both wants to share His perspective with us, so that we may grow up (see 1 Cor. 2:10-13).

When we become a prototype, and when the Holy Spirit begins to move in the Church in power, we also will come into a different level of warfare. We must understand this. If we are praying for power, we are unconsciously praying for battle. It makes sense now, doesn't it? If we are praying for anointing and power, we are unconsciously praying for battle and warfare, because that is what we will get. And along with power will come responsibility; along with power will come attack; along with power will come a level of warfare. If we are praying, "God, take us into a higher realm," we have to understand the dynamics of what we are requesting.

One of my mentors in the very early days of my life was a guy who was mentored by Smith Wigglesworth. This man would say to me, "Graham, never ever ask God for patience, because the Bible says tribulation works patience." So when you say, "Father, make me more patient," God listens to that prayer and says in reply, "I've got just what you need." Suddenly, our lives are full of trouble and we are thinking, *What did I do to deserve this? What is happening, Lord? Don't You love me anymore?* The Lord answers, "I am just answering your prayer." We are saying, "But I prayed for patience." He replies, "Yes, I know, and I am giving you the means to achieve it. Trouble works patience."

This dialogue begins in our heart because we begin to realize that prayer has consequences on both a conscious and unconscious level. When we pray for power, we are unconsciously asking God for warfare. It is in battle that God trains our hands for war, thus increasing our capacity for power.

If we pray, "Lord God, take us into a whole new realm of anointing" (which is a great prayer to pray, by the way), we have to be aware also of the unconscious factor that we are praying at the same time. Every time you go to a new level, you meet a new devil, and the devil on the next level will be stronger than the one on the current level. We need to fight against a strong devil to make us a strong church! This is how it works; we have to beat the devil on the first level before we go on to the next one.

Are you aware of those awful computer games that children play? I used to play these games with my children. Even my daughter could thrash me. In one particular computer game we had to pick up a number of things before we could get through the door into the next level. There were about six chances of getting killed while we were picking up about 14 or 15 different objects, beating off those opponents, and escaping on to the next level. I could never make it out of the first level.

In fact, my daughter, who was about eight at the time, could get through to level 12 and would look at me in absolute scorn. I said to her, "Oh, Sweetheart, Daddy is getting a bit old. I can't move my fingers fast enough." She said, "Daddy, the brain controls the fingers." Ouch, boy, is that perception or what? But I could never get out of the first level. And if I ever would have the opportunity to move on to the second level, I would have to pick up 30 objects and fight off 12 opponents who were bigger than those on the first level.

Every time you get to a new level you meet a new and stronger devil. At this point, God will give you more strength. The strength of the opponent determines the strength that God will give you to survive on that level. The strength and power that God wants you to have will be determined by the quality of the enemy coming against you.

The point is this: We have to beat the devil on the level that we are on. As we beat him and make him submit, he becomes our footstool that we can climb on to get into the next level. The first level is always about the flesh. The first rule of spiritual warfare is that we cannot take ground from the devil if he has got ground in us. So the first devil to beat is not the enemy—it is ourselves. Who was it who said, "We have met the enemy and he is us"? The first enemy we have to beat is our own flesh.

The first level of warfare is always spirit versus flesh. The first level of contact and activity in warfare is always about dying to self and learning how to live in the Holy Spirit.

Jesus said, *"The ruler of this world is coming, and he has nothing in Me"* (John 14:30b). The enemy's whole point of his temptation of Jesus was to get Him to act independently of God. The first battle is always against you, for we are partakers of the warfare that Jesus is always provoking.

The failure to understand the mind of the Lord in transition will have us running away at critical moments. If we have no revelatory rationale for current events, we will always interpret things in the realm of the soul rather than of the Spirit.

One particular year, I was working with a church that was going through a notably tough time of transition. There were repeated phone calls to my home in the United Kingdom, with several e-mails asking the same question: "Is there a word from God for us at this time?" It was not simply a word of prophecy that they were seeking, but insight that would help them progress.

I was due to be with them approximately five weeks after their first telephone call, and I continued to pray about their circumstances for several weeks without any illumination. Eventually, I arrived in their city. The elders met me at the airport with the same question on their lips, and I shook my head. Anticipating a hot shower and an early night after a horrendous transatlantic flight, I was amazed to be driven to the church instead where a meeting was in progress. The same question was on the lips of everyone I spoke to before and during the meeting. After a short time of worship, I was given the platform. I had nothing to say.

While praying the prayer of faith publicly, I simultaneously prayed the prayer of the desperate, silently. As we waited on the Lord together, I felt Him ask me to recall previous prophetic words over the church. We had gone through them over a year ago. (I believe that prophecy gives us a faith-agenda and a prayer-focus.)

All these words had been concerned with gaining ground, fighting spiritual warfare, training up champions, and being a militant church. I also remembered some of the wonderful prayers that I had enjoyed in this church—prayers of passion and sacrifice, prayers that revolved around a desperate need to see God glorified through their lives. I recalled how impressed I had been with the quality and fervor of their praying in previous times. Their prayers were also about asking for a warfare anointing for themselves and the region.

Then I felt the Lord breathe these words into my spirit: "These current difficulties are not the work of the enemy, though he is active. It is not the result of persecution, though there is human opposition at work. This is not real warfare; nor are they on any battlefield of note. This is their training ground, not a battleground. The word of the Lord is, 'Welcome to boot camp.' There is no word of deliverance. I am training them for the real battles to come. It is time to grow up and learn how to endure hardness as good soldiers of Jesus Christ (see 2 Tim. 2:3). This is not real warfare; it is training. I am toughening them up."

This did not go down well at all. As good soldiers, they had to fall in and stand up, not fall out and disappear. Until that moment, they had no revelatory rationale for what was happening, so they were at the mercy of an overactive imagination. They were ready to blame the enemy or point the finger at the leadership, the vision, and the church in general. When in trouble, the soul always wants a way out. The soul never likes to suffer and will always seek release if it can. If we have no revelation, the soul will interpret events to suit its own requirements. The spirit man, though, will always rest and wait until it hears God.

Understand the prayers you are praying. Reflect on the implications. Keep a log of prayers that you persist in. They will give you a valuable clue to the process you have embarked upon.

ORDER AND CHAOS

In the opening paragraph of his novel, *A Tale of Two Cities*, Charles Dickens begins with this narrative: "It was the best of times, it was the worst of times." This statement very accurately describes much of what we are experiencing in renewal and transition. There are so many wonderful things happening in the midst of real upheaval. At the point where vision is unfolding and we are reaching upward to see our destiny, the ground opens up beneath our feet and we find ourselves plunging headlong in the opposite direction. There is a divine contradiction at work here that we need to understand, for it will give us the real keys to incorporating transition and process.

Being part of a network of churches and having played a significant role in the transitional process of many churches, I believe that the Lord has given me some key insights into the nature, character, and methodology of transition. There is a pattern that the Lord is making known in these days.

God is in the business of enabling us to think and act like Him (see Isa. 55:8-9). We are learning how to make adjustments in this area. We are changing from being a spiritually dry, consuming Church that relies on the ministry of others to find their destiny, to becoming a living, breathing army of people who are productive and anointed.

Order is always preceded by chaos. Whenever God restores order, something is being birthed out of the chaos He allowed in the first place. Everything is part of the whole with God. We look at chaos and say, "This is not of God." The Bible, though, points to chaos and disagrees with us. In chaos, God disenfranchises the old order and births the new! Chaos is the overlap period between the old, unsuccessful, and now defunct period and the new model, pattern, and prototype that He is releasing in embryonic form. It is the establishing of this new type that brings order.

In Acts 2, we see the closing of the old system, which is Pharisaical, and the creation of a new prototype Church. There are 120 people in an upper room when the Holy Spirit falls, creating chaos. No one is sure about what is happening! Within the chosen group, though, there is order because they know they are the prototype promised by Jesus. Other people around them, however, see only the events, which they interpret as chaos.

Of course, it is true of human nature that if we are not a part of something and we do not understand it, we always want to criticize it. We criticize what we do not understand. During this time in Acts, there were people speaking in languages that they never learned, and there were people staggering about in the streets at an inappropriate time of day.

And then, the Bible says that Peter stood up to speak. Why did he have to stand up? Probably because he was lying down at the time! Everything looked so chaotic; most people's interpretation of events was that people were drunk in alcoholic excess (see Acts 2:13). On the contrary, people were staggering around under the influence of God. A new order of church was emerging in chaotic circumstances, which were the teething problems of bringing in something new, strange, and noisy. Everything was more than a little frantic.

This process is a viable part of transition and is best kept "in team" together. Do not be upset at the apparent chaos; rather, focus on the order that God is developing. At this level, church is messy. Most times, church is like a building site, and I have never seen a building site look clean and tidy (and I worked on several in my earlier years).

In one part, houses are being completed and lawns laid. In another, foundations are being laid in a hole in the ground. In between, we have mess and chaos with homes at varying stages of development. The church will resemble this process at times. Even if we have the blueprint for growth and change, we will make a mess before we create order and growth. In the midst of it all, we need to rejoice at all aspects of the building program. Take pleasure in the completion of the finished article, and rejoice that something new is beginning. If we can learn to see the good in most things, our perspective will be more faith-filled than negative.

Our problem is that we have lived with a certain kind of order in recent years. It is the order of human beings engaged in a work of God, but not understanding how He likes to work. Our version is sanitized and predictable. We build with our perspective on how it should happen, not actually how He likes to do it. His reality is not always to our liking. He is a facilitator more concerned with people growing than with organizational correctness.

God works His own brand of order in the midst of total chaos. The creation story gives us unprecedented insight into how He loves to work. In Genesis, we are told that the earth was in chaos. It was formless and void; the words used are *tohu bohu*. There you have it! A totally biblical expression for everything being a mess is *tohu bohu*! This is my friend Lance Walnau's expression for complete and utter confusion, disorder, and a perplexing muddle.

Often, it is our failure to live where God is living that prevents us from seeing the order that He is imprinting on the chaos He is allowing. God is so restful. He is the essence of rest, totally at peace. His Son, Jesus, is called the Prince of Peace because He manifested rest at every opportunity and created peace around Himself. During the storm on the lake, He stood amidst fearful and anxious disciples and spoke out of who He was. He was totally unworried, and it showed.

Like the worried disciples with Jesus asleep in the boat, we often gain the impression that God may not care. In the midst of chaos, God is frequently silent. Why is He so quiet and silent? I think it is because He is teaching us how to rest in Him. He whispers so that we need to become quiet ourselves just to hear His voice. He speaks in a still small voice because He is teaching us stillness and truth. In Psalm 46, the psalmist begins with an earthquake and ends with, *"Be still, and know that I am God."* In chaos, God is bringing stillness and order!

The Lord operates from stillness. Whatever boat you are storming through at the moment, He is on that same boat wanting you to grow up enough to call on His peace. God does not create order out of order; He creates order only out of chaos. He takes the order that we have established around our ministry, and He injects it with new vision and purpose. This new depth of call will lead us to a place of vulnerability and inadequacy. This is a form of chaos because it removes the certainties that we are familiar with, thus creating a greater dependency upon God Himself.

Each new level of anointing and power demands a fresh understanding of process. Learning about the process of transition will teach us how to wait for the proceeding Word of God—the "let there be" word that creates order out of our current perplexity. The process that God prefers broadly follows the creative genius He displays in the Genesis transition.

The light of His word then breaks into the confusion of our combined thinking and experience. Our rationale is expanded as we come to grips with fresh faith and insight. We begin to see different results as the word becomes real in our experience, and there is heavenly interaction as we line up behind the purposes of God. The anointing grows into a lifestyle of walking before God at this new perception and participation.

Revelation then leads to expansion. Subsequently, expansion creates a solid faith foundation for a new level of productivity with the Lord. Interaction with the Holy Spirit leads us to a whole new anointing and lifestyle as we learn to rest in the Lord in this advanced dimension of the Spirit. In all of this process, we find the Holy Spirit brooding over the Church, enjoying the *tohu bohu*, and breathing life into us as we submit to the work of God in transition.

The point is, we cannot hold on to our order and still progress to a new level of anointing. When a new paradigm unfolds before us, it will always take us back to zero. Paradigms do not build on one another; they replace each other. We start again with a new dependency arising out of fresh inadequacy. Our dependency upon the Lord has to go to deeper levels before our experience can rise to new heights. This is transition!

When it is necessary, the Lord will stand up in our boat and speak peace to our situation. Peace comes from the anointing with the word that the Spirit releases to us. One hundred twenty people were having an orderly prayer meeting when the Holy Spirit blew in and created disorder and some confusion. Now, God is not the author of confusion (see 1 Cor. 14:33); however, if we do not have His perspective on the current situation, then we are confused! Many people are confused because they have little patience to stop and listen to God. We want to hear what we feel we need to know to get relief in our situation. We are committed more at times to our comfort than we are to our development.

The Lord, on the other hand, is committed to giving us comfort in the midst of our obedience to Him in transition.

People were confused in the Acts 2 account because they did not know what God was doing. We often naively think that if the Lord is in something, there won't be any confusion. That was clearly not the case here. Frequently, God's action when entering a situation brought puzzlement. We see bewildered people throughout the Scriptures from Abraham to Paul. That is precisely because God, when He intervenes, brings a new order. A violent, rushing wind blew everyone off their feet and disrupted the meeting, resulting in people staggering about in the street where they were accused of being drunk. There was joy and laughter and the confusion of many different languages, leaving many people scratching their heads in wonderment (see Acts 2:1-13). Interestingly, it was God's order that turned the community upside down!

First, there was confusion in the church until they came into alignment with what God was doing. Then their obedience and new participation created confusion in the world (who thinks the church is predictable!) and this turned society upside down and inside out—to the point where people dared not join the church, but could not stay away either! Confusing, isn't it?

We have managed, with all our knowledge, experience, and understanding, to make the church into a stereotype. Many churches can function quite well (at a low level) without God. But the world sees us in our independence and assumes that we are just a stereotype organization. They put us neatly into a box so they can dismiss us as irrelevant.

The Lord is now blowing that box apart. He is dismantling the stereotypes and creating new prototypes of church, and we are being made uncomfortable with the Lord. He is creates a divine imbalance to promote dependency upon Him. However, as we come into alignment with His present purpose, the world will become uncomfortable with us. Then they will become, in turn, either antagonistic or fascinated by what the Lord is doing. We will become a talking point for all the right reasons. Transition leads to revival, which is effective and persecuted, and definitely not ignored!

There is also something else happening that we must understand. There are times when everything we try to do does not work. There is a resistance. None of our meetings, attempts at outreach, new initiatives in prayer, or youth work seem to work. People become more discouraged, and as a church, we fast and pray. We blame it on the enemy and try to identify the enemy resisting us.

Perhaps, though, it is not entirely the work of the enemy. Possibly, the resistance is not external, but internal. It could be that our wineskin is the real problem. Perhaps God is trying to break the mold so that He can bring us into a new dimension of power and activity. We might be trying to do new things out of the old structure, which is resisting us. If our structure does not work for us, it will not work for non-believers coming to us. If our wineskin is not releasing the full blessing of God for our members, then nonmembers will not be persuaded to try it. Wine turned to vinegar will not find a palate!

KNOW THE OPPOSITION

The ground of transition will be contested by an implacable enemy who will try and frustrate us at every turn. That is why the whole point of times of transition is to increase our dependency upon the Lord. We must learn how to hold on to the majesty and supremacy of Jesus.

It is so easy when we are going through change and transition to blame the enemy, to blame people, or to look at human rationale for our situation. However, I believe that God wants to give us a divine rationale because, in my experience with God—limited though it may be—I have come to understand that He allows in His wisdom what He could easily prevent by His power. If God is allowing certain things, then we want to know His wisdom. Our prayer, however, may be more geared to asking Him to stop the situation than to help us understand it. When God chooses to ignore our prayer, we have to ask another question or make a different prayer—one that may be more in line with what God is doing. That is why we need the wisdom to know the difference.

God is speaking deep-to-deep these days. Jesus said to His disciples, *"I still have many things to say to you, but you cannot bear them now"* (John 16:12). In other words, He was limited in what He could do in their hearts and what He could speak into their lives because of their own perception. The Lord is always trying to raise our perception of what He is doing. That is what we call *revelation*.

That could be said of the Church right now. Deep is calling to deep. I have never known a time when I have felt such a weight of Heaven pressing in on what we are doing. Angelic sightings around the world are on the increase. Demonic manifestations that are more powerful and bizarre are also on the rise. The supernatural is folding itself layer upon layer on top of the natural with Heaven desperate to come to earth. There are more intercessors now in the earth than there have ever been in the whole of the Church's entire history.

There is a tremendous amount of powerful intercession going up these days. Many churches, no matter how small, have someone praying intensely. It is easy to see that the whole world of what we are doing is shifting. There are deep things happening across the Church, some of which we don't yet understand. In addition, I believe there will be some messages coming to the Church by angelic visitation because we won't be able to bear the weight of them. No one will be able to bear the weight of revelation by himself from the Holy Spirit. I believe that we will have angels coming just as we saw in the Scriptures, in both the Old and New Covenants.

Angels are heralds of eternity sent to help mankind break through when they cannot break out. They operate at the points where Heaven touches the earth, where significance needs to be broadcast, and where God's plans and purposes need to unfold with dynamic effect. They are unlooked-for occurrences. One cannot summon an angel; they do only the bidding of God. They are ministering spirits sent to give a message or support at a critical time. Their presence is increasing in the earth, and this is a truly supernatural time for churches to gain that heavenly cutting edge of spiritual gifting and character.

We are breaking new ground and becoming more prophetic in a world going mad with reason. Prophetic churches pass through things ahead of time, which makes for a target of criticism. This will no doubt be good for our humility. Human opposition is designed by God to bring us into grace, while demonic opposition brings us into greater power. All opposition is designed for our benefit.

Human opposition will teach us how to be gracious and merciful. We will learn how to love our enemies, how to pray for people who persecute us, and how to bless those who work against us.

Demonic opposition is to teach us how to stand in the authority and the power of the Lord Jesus. It is designed to show us the majesty and supremacy of Jesus and to enable us to learn how to submit to God (see James 4:7-8).

A prophetic church will pay a price to see the prophetic emerge in the earth. Everything that this type of church does is built on progressive truth. Revelation that is unfolding will not be understood by other churches until it is fleshed out in something visible. This takes perseverance on our behalf, so that one day our critics can have fellowship with us in spirit and truth. We need to keep praying over our detractors, that the Lord will open their eyes, that what is invisible and therefore incomprehensible can be seen and apprehended. The Church needs a total change of perspective to operate in the supernatural realm. We cannot indulge in the laws of reason and logic and expect to fight off the demonic. We cannot hear words concerning the future without willingly changing our practices in the present.

We will see what God is seeing; speak out what He is saying; and do what only He is doing—simply because He wills it. We will have to suspend our disbelief to share the perceptions of the Holy Spirit.

At the same time, the enemy must be known, isolated, and overcome if we are to move into the realms of God that are unfolding. That is why we need the prophetic. Prophets have a profound love of God and a deep hatred of the enemy. They have always been in the forefront of any battle against untruth, deception, injustice, and oppression.

Most of the leaders in the Bible had a strong prophetic dimension to their lives. Many were prophets! Yet the notion in today's churches is that prophets and leadership do not mix (work that one out). We have a church that does not understand process and growth, largely because the people who understand these realms are not in any place of authority or real influence. Reason has replaced revelation.

I love reason. I believe that God is reasonable, except when He chooses not to be. Then we need revelation. Words of wisdom are meant to provide us with supernatural reasoning that is not grounded in human logic and intelligence.

The mind must be renewed at times in order to keep pace with God's reasoning. Things that do not make sense in the natural will unfold supernaturally by divine revelation as God communicates at a deeper level of faith and on a higher plane of thought. Our thoughts are not His...yet!

Real prophetic people (that is, those who have been disciplined and shaped) intuitively interact with God on this level of supernatural understanding by revelation. Real apostles (that is, fathers, master builders, and facilitators) have the innate capacity in the Spirit to interpret prophetic revelation into a strategy for church response and development. That is why the new prototype of church will be founded on the partnership between apostles and prophets dependent on the Lord Jesus Christ.

FRUSTRATION RELEASES IMPARTATION

Very few people understand the process of turning prophetic potential into something actual. It is one matter to have received a prophetic word; it is quite another to see it fulfilled. I personally know many individuals and churches with significant prophetic words spoken over them, but remember that all *personal* prophecy is conditional, whether or not any conditions are implied or stated in the prophecy itself. Conditional prophecy relates to the possibility, not the inevitability of fulfillment. It can be delayed or even canceled according to our response as well as by our capacity to align our hearts and lives in lifestyle obedience to the revealed Word of God in the Scriptures. There is also unconditional prophecy, which relates to God's overall plan for mankind. It may be adjusted but can never be prevented from coming to pass because it depends upon God Himself, not human response.

We need perseverance and patience to walk with God and see that word fulfilled according to the Lord's discretion and timing, as well as according to our preparation and placement. We will need to work with the Holy Spirit to turn our potential into reality.

Working with frustration is a key factor in turning our potential into something actual. I like frustrated people. They are one of the hopes of the Church. Most people are frustrated because they care about something. However, they have a distinct responsibility to the Holy Spirit to use their frustration for the correct purpose. It is sent to provoke them to intercession. They must allow the Holy Spirit to direct their frustration into meaningful prayer and waiting on God. In this way, by the Spirit, frustration is turned into passion, which releases the prophetic to empower people before God.

If people abuse their relationship with the Holy Spirit, their frustration is used by the flesh to sow discord, strife, and division. They become a dissenting voice rather than a positive prophetic utterance. Frustration will reveal our true heart and release an impartation that is either negative and destructive, or positive and empowering.

If we intervene between our frustration and God's purpose, we are tampering with the law of cause and effect. People often do not guard their thoughts carefully enough, especially when under the pressure of frustration. When we leave our thoughts unguarded, the flesh can usurp what the Lord wants to do. We must understand the power of frustration if we are to avoid mis-creation. We need a genuine respect for cause and effect as a necessary condition for turning frustration into impartation.

By choosing God's purpose, we reject the potential for divisiveness to occur. Cause always belongs to God; the effect is whatever is released through the Son. Frustration is sent first to change us, to make us more into the image of Jesus; that is cause and effect, stage one. Stage two occurs when we allow frustration to cause us to stand in the gap and intercede for others, the effect of which is a release of impartation that empowers and inspires. Stage three occurs only through the success of the first two phases. That is, we arrive at a place of trustworthy servanthood after having passed the test of unselfishness.

The fundamental conflict in the world is between creation and mis-creation. All love is implicit in the first, and all fear is implicit in the second. The conflict is therefore between love and fear.

Do we love God enough to allow Him to fulfill His purpose no matter how much it hurts ours? Do we love other people enough to serve and help them no matter how much we want to be right? Alternatively, are we more afraid of not being recognized or proven right in this issue? Are we afraid that we will be treated just like a servant? If we have ever asked the Lord for the privilege to be His servant, then we really must not get upset if He treats us like one!

Isaac was not the cause of Abraham's prophetic inheritance to be fulfilled; he was the effect. The cause to fulfill the prophecy over Abraham was only ever going to be God Himself (see Gen. 18:10-19). Part of our frustration too is that we cannot see where our lives fit into the current circumstances unless they change. Therefore, in acting within the issue, we also are trying to create space for ourselves. We have an ulterior motive, no matter how we dress it up to hide it. Hidden agendas, no matter how benign, will inevitably lead to a mis-creation of God's purpose. Be assured that the significant test in frustration is to determine whether we will sacrifice what is close to our own heart in order to serve God. Can we lay our desire and our hope for significance on the altar of God and trust in Him alone to fulfill it?

It is a test—a real and great examination of our motives, desires, and true spirit of servanthood. It is here that we will discover whether we will usurp the occasion for our own ends or whether we will lay down our lives for the purpose of obedience. When Abraham was told to offer up Isaac as a sacrifice, it was a major test of his obedience (see Gen. 22). He went believing that *"God will provide for Himself the lamb for a burnt offering..."* (Gen. 22:8b).

He had the knife in his hand ready to kill what was most dear to him, before the Lord stopped him. The blessing and impartation that were released at this time to Abraham were both huge for himself and momentous for those coming after him (see Gen. 22:15-18).

We can hold on to our own dream only by letting it go in the service of God. That, perhaps, is one of the lessons of frustration that we all must learn if we are to be true servants of God. His promise and goodness are the cause of our fulfillment, not our desire to take hold of the promise and make it work.

David had to learn a similar lesson in his life with Saul. King Saul had pursued David with every evil intent to prevent his son-in-law from becoming his successor to the throne. When Saul entered the very cave where David and his men were hiding, to relieve himself, he was at their mercy. David's friends urged him to kill Saul, believing that God had ordained it. But on that day, David realized that the cause of his inheriting the throne was not the demise of Saul. It was simply the will and power of God to fulfill His own word. The only person who could wreck the cause of God was David himself (see 1 Sam. 24).

In frustration, conflict is inevitable if we are not focused upon God's purpose. Our self-righteous flesh will rise up to prove its point, justifying itself in the process. The effect of our flesh is then unproductive and damaging to the cause of God. Therefore, in frustration we must be ready with our obedience to fulfill the cause of God. Then the effect of our frustration will become an impartation of encouragement, prophecy, insight, and blessing. Readiness is a prerequisite for accomplishment.

As soon as a state of readiness occurs within us, it will be accompanied by a desire to accomplish the will of God through His Spirit. Readiness is the beginning of confidence. God knows what He is doing, and we would be much better off to trust His faithfulness to do it than our capacity to understand it.

We know that all things become clear in the end. The God who will not explain Himself before the event will reveal His purpose after we have trusted. He does not always speak initially, but He always speaks eventually. By submitting to Him, no matter how we feel, we become ready to do His will.

Frustration is either the spark of life that creates a new dimension or the detonation of all that we hold dear. Be careful not to snuff out that spark, but nurture it properly. The current problems that frustrate leadership concern time, motion, and efficiency. With so many things happening, and with so many claims on our time, it is easier and seemingly more effective (in terms of results) to police certain situations and people than it is to facilitate and develop them. It is easier to deny than to expedite.

People need to understand that, first, frustration is an internal matter. It will highlight where and how the Lord wants to change the individual. Leaders need to give them help primarily to rid the people of unhelpful elements. As David requested, *"Search me, O God, and know my heart; try me, and know my anxieties; and see if there is any wicked way in me, and lead me in the way everlasting"* (Ps. 139:23-24).

We must ensure that our anxiety (frustration) about something is not turned into anything hurtful to others. Once we have allowed the Lord to deal with our own hearts, we are free to pray effectively and to stand in the gap for others. People who want to complain and have negative fellowship rather than pray do not understand that they are failing their own test to legitimize their ministry. How we deal with our frustration is a major test of our faithfulness to working with the Holy Spirit. Can He trust us? Are we committed to the fruit of the Holy Spirit or just His gifting? Are we committed to the building up of the Body or to just our own ministry?

Frustration is an elegant test to determine faithfulness and current attitude. It is a privilege to be frustrated. It means, if we handle it properly, if we prove out and achieve what is on God's heart, that a new door in the Spirit realm will open up to us. If we miss the opportunity and our frustration falls into fleshly activity, that door will close on us, and it may be some time before the Lord will trust us enough to open that door again. Frustration is the potential to grow and develop.

Of course, if we are constantly and continuously frustrated, we will need some form of counseling and possibly deliverance from spiritual negativity, pride, contempt, and arrogance. The flesh will have gotten the better of us on a regular basis until we become a liability. The enemy, not the Holy Spirit, is then monitoring our frustration for the purpose of strife and division, not growth and development.

Through our frustration, God will change us first; then He will change people around us. Frustration will bring everyone and everything into alignment with God's purpose, if we submit to Him. There are two things we really need here. First, we need a revelation of what frustration is really all about. Second, we must understand that transition is the place where revelation becomes experience to us. Transition is a testing and proving ground. It is the place between promise and fulfillment where we are tested to see if we can inhabit the place that God wants to give us.

The promise made to Adam was that he would rule over the earth and have dominion in it. He was put into the Garden of Eden to see if he could rule over himself. The garden was his transition place—a smaller sphere of influence and activity that was designed to be his testing and proving ground. He missed it.

We must be honest with ourselves. How many times have we been frustrated? Has anything positive and remarkable ever occurred in those times? If we are blaming others, we have missed the point. For every finger we point at someone else, there are three pointing back at us.

Did those times of frustration lead us to greater impartation, renewed servanthood, or a test passed with flying colors? If not, then these tests will come again. Times of testing are part of the process of turning our potential into something actual. We can tell who are men and women of real substance in God. They are the ones at peace with themselves. They own nothing and yet possess all things. They are not striving, not promoting themselves. They are content to trust God, and He puts things into their hands because He trusts them. Their frustration has been redeemed, and in its place is a continuous flow of impartation. They have become facilitators for other people, for they are not concerned with their own place in the scheme of things. Great servants always have a place. Faithfulness is its own reward.

RECOGNIZING A BREAKTHROUGH

Breakthroughs are not always obvious. Many do not recognize their point of origin. They are like the "magic eye" pictures that we see in retail stores. On the surface, all we see is a mass of multicolored dots. However, when we concentrate and focus on looking beyond the surface, the picture hidden beneath materializes.

Breakthroughs do not begin at the point of discovery. They start much further back than we imagine. They begin at the point where we set ourselves to seek the Lord by extended, intensive prayer with fasting. Consider Daniel who had been praying, fasting, and mourning intensely for three weeks (see Dan. 10:2-4). At the end of this time, he received a visitation from an angel, who spoke these words to him:

> *Do not fear, Daniel, for from the first day that you set your heart to understand, and to humble yourself before your God, your words were heard; and I have come because of your words* (Daniel 10:12).

Daniel was not aware of the breakthrough or its point of origin until he was told about it. Breakthroughs occur when we begin to pray in earnest, and they are recognized after prayer is complete. Daniel stood firm in prayer so that his intercession could be completed before the Lord. Had he given up on prayer, that which had begun on the first day of intercession may not have been completed to the point of recognition at a later time.

Everything that God does is birthed through warfare and confrontation. While Daniel was praying, warfare was being conducted over the nation, although Daniel was unaware of the battle or even his part in it. He had no idea what his faithful praying had contributed to the heavenly battle.

Wherever Jesus went, He provoked warfare. Demons would cry out, provoked by His presence. Healing and deliverance then occurred because of the interaction between His presence and demonic forces. Some people tried to stone Him, others kill Him. Likewise, if we are praying for His presence to come, provocation will come with Him! We will partake of all the warfare He provokes.

One day, I received a phone call from a church leader who said, "We really want you to come." He continued to extend this invitation over several months, and finally I said, "Why do you keep pursuing this? Tell me a bit about your history." He replied, "We need a breakthrough." I said, "Well, are you ready for a breakthrough?" He said, "We need some blessing to cause us to break through." I answered, "I am sorry, but no one breaks through in blessing. You break through only in confrontation."

I went on, "Blessing gives us breadth; confrontation gives us depth. Real breakthroughs don't come in times of blessing. They come in times of warfare and confrontation. If you want me to come to give you breakthrough, you had better know that if you don't have a confrontation while I am there, you will have it soon after I have gone, because that is the nature of breakthrough. You will need to experience a battle to break through. You have to be engaged in a war to break through. The enemy must come against you so that you can break through against him.

"There has to be interaction between the Holy Spirit in you and the enemy. So if you want to break through, you must understand that it will arise out of the confrontation between God and the devil among your people. Your steadfast spirit will be the main reason that breakthrough occurs. If you quit, breakthrough will not happen. The art of breakthrough is learning to live with the God of war."

In times of war, we will see a side of God that we do not see at any other time. That is why confrontation and warfare are so important. We are not afraid of it; the truth is, we have to learn to like it. That doesn't mean that we all become deliriously happy at the thought of spiritual warfare. Warfare is a sober business. We can relish the fight once we are in it, but we must count the cost before we start it. Our God is not afraid of anything; nor is He upset or provoked by anything. He is a God of war and He laughs in the face of His enemy, because God knows who He is in Himself. He has total knowledge of His own identity.

And He wants to put all the qualities and characteristics of His own warfaring nature into the Church. However, He establishes them in us only on the battlefield. Therefore, we must get on the battlefield! Yet there are a lot of churches that are not even on the battlefield yet because they aren't good enough to be attacked by the devil. Most churches are not good enough to come into real spiritual warfare. The enemy does not have to attack them because they do a pretty good job of attacking themselves!

The devil can simply come in and press a few buttons of the flesh: resentment, bitterness, ambition, pride, arrogance, and unteachable behavior. And as long as he can continue to press those buttons, we will never make it to the same battlefield. We must win the internal battle as individuals before we can win the external one, and we also have to win it on a corporate level so that we come together as one people with one heart, one mind, and one voice. Then we are ready for real warfare, and then all hell will break loose around us. Subsequently, we will find that God will reveal Himself in a way that we never thought possible. The nature and spiritual capacity of a church changes dramatically when the God of battle presents Himself in its midst!

Jesus said these words in Luke 22:28-30:

But you are those who have continued with Me in My trials. And I bestow upon you a kingdom, just as My Father bestowed one upon Me, that you may eat and drink at My table in My kingdom, and sit on thrones judging the twelve tribes of Israel.

"You are those who have continued with Me in My trials." There is an anointing for fellowship with God in confrontation that births a bestowing of Kingdom in our hearts. Kingdom is given to us in the violence of confrontation. The Kingdom of Heaven suffers violence, and the violent take it by force (see Matt. 11:12). We need a godly violence in our heart that says, "We are not going to be moved; this is what we believe in. We are going to stand here; we are not moving. We are standing here, and we are believing God."

In warfare and seasons of trouble, there is a quality of suffering and perseverance that actually births in us a greater anointing to work the works of God. God actually trusts us, because He trusts what He sees of suffering inside our heart and life.

We cannot build anything without suffering, yet so many leaderships are moving away from suffering. Good leadership knows how to suffer; they know about patience and perseverance to stand their ground. People can leave, but the leaders will stand their ground. It is in that time that God learns He can trust us. He bestows something in us. Anytime God has actually increased the anointing upon my life (over the past 20 years), it has come after a time of severe battle, warfare, criticism, or suffering of one kind or another. And then, we suddenly look back and we realize that the grace of God helped us to stand in that time. The blessing of God came upon us afterwards and even increased the anointing. Paul said, *"I thank Christ Jesus our Lord who has enabled me, becaused He counted me faithful, putting me into the ministry"* (1 Tim. 1:12). There is a faithfulness there that we are both earning and learning to develop in the heart of the Lord.

Each one of us will go through that kind of transition, and we need to understand the stages that God will take us through so that we don't run at the critical moment. We will experience some interesting and critical times in church life where everything is balanced on a knife's edge. But we will also learn about the mind of God as He teaches us to walk by faith and not by sight. In addition, we will receive His goodness and mercy. His mouth will discipline us into the simple obedience of faith while His heart will comfort us in our distress of learning.

God will speak to our mind when we have sinned and say, " *'Come now, and let us reason together,' says the Lord, 'though your sins are like scarlet, they shall be as white as snow...'"* (Isa. 1:18). The remainder of the time He will say, *"Trust in the Lord with all your heart, and lean not on your own understanding"* (Prov. 3:5). The issue is if we believe, not if we understand.

In the next dimension of church, we must prepare ourselves to walk with the God of the unreasonable. He will call us to do the impossible, to take on prophetic projects that are inconceivable to our mind-sets. Therefore, we must nurture the prophetic gift and ministry in our midst. Without it, we cannot become a prophetic church that is able to envision all that the Lord would want to accomplish in and through us.

Without that revelatory rationale to guide and help us, we will miss the grandeur of the wider purposes of God. We will be trying to take a neighborhood while He wants to give us the city. We will be attempting to believe God about the wider locality when He wants to use us as a catalyst to take the nation.

When our own thinking has the upper mind, we interpret everything with soulish logic. We look at our own resources and the scale of the problem in front of us, and we make a rational, intelligent judgment of our chances for pulling it off. Then, if the circumstances look too huge and awesome, we will not even attempt the matter. We will be like the ten spies who returned from spying in Canaan. We will give an "evil report" of what the opposition is like and of our chances of victory (see Num. 13:25-33).

However, when we are moving in faith regarding God's ability, we put a different complexion on things. Like Joshua and Caleb, we will give a report that is full of regard for the anointing of God, even at our own expense:

> *The land we passed through to spy out is an exceedingly good land. If the Lord delights in us, then He will bring us into this land and give it to us, "a land which flows with milk and honey." Only do not rebel against the Lord, nor fear the people of the land, for they are our bread; their protection has departed from them, and the Lord is with us. Do not fear them* (Numbers 14:7b-9).

There are some bold faith proclamations here:

1) If the Lord is pleased with us, He will give us the land.
2) Do not fear the people of the land, for they will be our prey.
3) Their protection has been removed, and the Lord is with us!

These two men did not deny the truth of the bad report; there were giants, fortified cities, and a strong army. But Joshua and Caleb focused on the Lord and His power. The other spies did the opposite and felt insignificant and incapable as a result.

Being a prophetic church means that we live by every word that God speaks into our current situation, as it happens. We do not live on previous words, but *proceeding* ones.

There is a revelatory rationale for all that God does. In transition, He is working to prepare us for the next dimension of life in the Spirit.

There is a process to follow and understand, and there is a break-through that comes with transition. Unfortunately, many churches will not survive the transition and will break up under the pressure. Transition is the sternest test in a church's history. Only the best will take hold of their inheritance in the next stage. But beware—the pass mark is not what we think it is!

There are four stages to transition. First is *revelation*, which is the unfolding of God's vision and purpose. This will plunge us headlong into *confrontation* with the enemy, as the flesh wars with the Spirit within. During this dilemma, God is doing a work of *transformation* to make us into the image of Christ. Only as the result of this process is seen can the final part, *manifestation*, be revealed. This is the unfolding and fulfilling of the initial revelation that began the season of transition. We will look at these stages in more detail in the next chapter.

Chapter Eleven

CHARACTER AND TRANSITION — PART TWO

C HURCHES are in transition for a variety of reasons. Some are changing from being an excellent local church to having a resource church anointing. This means an increase of vision and a new dimension of influence as more and more people are empowered and released. Others are gearing up into a regional context because they have a Kingdom heart that wants to see the city and the area move into a higher supernatural level.

Some churches are becoming apostolic centers where the resident fivefold ministries enable the Church to have an international significance in church planting and development.

For many churches, though, transition will simply mean the process by which they embrace their corporate destiny at a much higher level. Changes can be highlighted both onward and upward as we follow the proceeding word of God spoken over the work.

Let's look at the first of the four stages of transition: revelation, confrontation, transformation, and manifestation.

REVELATION

When the Lord seeks to move us into a new realm, He looks for us to have an increase of vision, anointing, and power. Along with that, there needs to come an increase of commitment and character.

The process of transition always begins with revelation, which is an insight from the Holy Spirit, possibly by prophetic disclosure. A prophetic word is released that inspires and ignites fresh faith regarding our destiny and overall vision as a church. The prophetic word may gather up previous words together with our current vision and take the whole concept much further forward. Revelation has impact. It will force us to reexamine where we are now and where we are going.

Revelation brings appraisal and scrutiny to everything we have done and are currently doing. Revelation gets under our skin, making us feel excited about what is opening up to us in the future, but also apprehensive about what it all means. Revelation means change. It is a beginning preceded by an ending (which is the paradox of transition), a closure and a new beginning, surrounded by vulnerability in the whole church.

The prophetic word makes us feel great. We become excited by the vision but sobered by the change involved.

Revelation may come by teaching. I have known several churches where new vision has arisen in the congregation because of expository teaching on the new church of the 21st century or new models of church. The members of that body have been caught up in faith to believe for and desire urgently to become such a church, and the teaching has been a catalyst to create a different environment within, where the members begin discussion and dialogue about structural changes, new vision, and a different spiritual culture.

I have known some churches where various people across the spiritual spectrum of the work have had almost identical dreams. The dreams have been about moving to a new location, starting a new project, developing a range of new church initiatives, or a mixture of such actions.

In several places, people had dreams that followed and built up a picture of what God was revealing from one person to another. In one instance, two of the nine people who had the same dream were actually in relational disharmony, and this event brought reconciliation! What has been interesting in these events has been the diversity of people used by the Lord. The emotional makeup, character, and relationship between these people have been markedly different. That fact itself has given serious weight to the supernatural quality of the event.

Of course, we do not change things based solely on dreams (although there is scriptural precedent to do so). However, we do use them as a catalyst for prayer, discussion, and further seeking of the Lord. We can recognize that God has sovereignly intervened, and now we need to make ourselves available to the Holy Spirit and one another.

Revelation also can come through apostolic insight and relationship. Many times there is an apostolic/prophetic visionary and a directive nature and quality to our discussions and relationship with our network friends and churches within c.net, the Cornerstone network to which I belong.

We care and pray for one another. We stand together in times of tension and difficulty; we work side by side in the Kingdom, teaching, imparting, ministering to one another, and wanting the best for one another. These all act as a catalyst for fresh direction and insight into vision and destiny. Apostles can interpret events surrounding a church and give practical wisdom regarding a way forward.

As a network, we like to perform church surveys from time to time within the family of churches. This helps us prevent churches from becoming stale and stereotyped. It tells us which churches are on the move and perhaps need prophetic encouragement. It tells us which churches may need overhaul in terms of their structure and mission.

We would expect revelation to flow out of these encounters, so that we can move forward with prayerful purpose. Revelation increases expectancy in the hearts of people, which is excellent and hopefully contagious, but it also creates problems for us in the outworking of new vision. We want our people to be in faith and have confidence in the Lord, and we want this new anticipation and excitement to touch as many as possible. But we must take care not to hype it up into something beyond what the Lord has spoken. Leaders often can go too far and turn anticipation into assumption in order to gather support for the new thing. If we can maintain a fair balance between excited vision and sober challenge, we will do well.

RHYTHM WITHOUT THE BLUES

Total balance is a myth. The only time we are completely balanced is when we stand still. Walking occurs when we throw our weight between one foot and another and maintain our momentum in a sense of direction. Spiritual balance is the movement of obedience and the distribution of faith between vision and sacrifice as we move together in unison. Expectancy can be dangerous for us if we are unfamiliar with how the Lord likes to work.

Although vision and revelation combine to bring us a fresh sense of destiny, they also can inhibit our capacity for thoughtful preparation. Jesus tells us in stark terms to count the cost of any new thing before we attempt it (see Luke 14:28-32). We can get caught up in the excitement and go-for-it attitude, only to get caught out when something opposite happens. Hype invalidates reflection. Assumption derides consideration.

Faith and caution are not in opposition. They are compatible soul mates—opposites attracted to the same God. Faith wants to go for it! Caution wants to do it right. Faith says, "Yes! We're going to do it." Caution says, "This is how we should go about it." Caution brings strategy to the impetus of faith so that nothing is wasted. The main difference between the two is pace. Faith wants to get there immediately; caution wants to get there in one piece! Faith will pay the cost, whatever it is; caution does not want to pay more than necessary. Faith says, "Let's just pay it as we go." Caution says, "Let's budget for it before we start!" Caution and faith need one another.

Without faith, caution will deliver a peacetime budget in a warfare situation. Without caution, faith will not have the strategy to overcome obstacles.

Faith believes it can run a marathon and can't wait to start running. Caution knows how to run a marathon so that faith doesn't run out of steam.

All runners will physically hit what is known in athletic circles as "the wall" in the marathon. But it is those who run with caution and belief allied together who will survive the worst obstacles and finish the race.

Faith plus caution is the marriage of particular knowledge and confident belief. Knowledge in this instance is the understanding of God's ways with a grasp of strategy and momentum. Everything has a rhythm in God. When He changes the momentum, the strategy must alter. Faith goes with the movement and momentum; caution goes with the rhythm and strategy. If we can connect together in this way, we will have rhythm without the blues!

The Lord will always make sure that every group has a mixture of these people within its membership. They are opposites in perception, but necessary allies in operation. This is the balance we must seek, the friendly interaction between faith and caution that allows us to run with patience the next stage of the great race. Faith is not mindless, nor caution faithless. They are the left and the right leg of movement. We need to understand them both and get them moving together if we are to avoid doing splits!

PROPHECY AND CONTRADICTION

There is a reason for this partnership. Expectation on its own will speed up our momentum to the point of launching out into the atmosphere. We may be happy to boldly go where no church has gone before in our lifetime. Expectation searches out the horizon and seeks to get to the high point of anointing and power as quickly as possible.

However, with God, at this stage the quality of the launching pad is more important than the actual rockets. We should spend time and energy making sure our rockets (faith and resources) can enable us to reach our destination (vision). The Lord seeks primarily to ensure that our launch base (character) is adequately upgraded to be able to handle the pressure of the new launch.

In expectation, we are thinking horizon, but God is thinking about foundation. When revelation comes, we want to get there as quickly as possible. We are enlivened by the prophetic power that captivates our hearts. However, there is a contradiction in the prophetic that declares to us, "You cannot get there (horizon) from here."

Contradiction is the journey from revelation to manifestation—the process of transition. Joseph received a prophetic dream that he would one day have authority above his father and brothers (see Gen. 37). The dream concerned them all bowing down to him. This prophecy was fulfilled eventually in Genesis 47, but not before the opposite had occurred. After relating the dreams to his family, instead of *them* looking up at *him*, Joseph found *himself* in a pit looking up at *them*!

He was sold as a slave and sent in chains to a distant country. His life had gone in the opposite direction to what he perhaps was expecting. Plainly, the Lord was not going to fulfill the prophecy over some empty-headed young man who did not have the sense to keep his mouth shut around some very irate brethren! After the calling comes the training. Once we have received serious prophetic input into our lives, we then need particular development before the word can be moved to a place of fulfillment.

David found a similar set of circumstances at work in his own life. He was anointed to be king by the prophet Samuel (see 1 Sam. 16), but nothing said or done at that time disclosed to David that he would be discredited and have to live in caves in the wilderness before the prophet's words came true.

Israel received a strong prophetic word from Moses (see Exod. 6:6-8) that contained seven "I will" declarations from the Lord regarding their future and their destiny. The words, however, never mentioned their journey into the wilderness or their subsequent testing by God as part of the means of fulfillment.

This is the major part of the transitional and prophetic process. Before our destiny can be fulfilled, we must conform to all the character requirements that are a priority if we are to represent the God of Heaven. He wants all of us to conform to the image of Jesus as a prerequisite to fulfillment of prophecy. After the initial excitement of the word and the release of vision and destiny, God switches His attention to our character. Now He has to work on our personality, nature, and temperament, to elevate it to the point of approved trustworthiness. Our destiny is put on hold until the time that we are proved out in our character.

After the prophecy, we are often immediately starstruck with our destiny; however, the Lord is looking at something different! He is looking at our character and gauging the work and development we will need in order to develop us to that place of high calling. This development will include a testing of our humility; our servant heart; our reliability under pressure; our truthfulness and purity; our leadership or ministry ability; our capacity to endure stress in warfare; our ability to learn from our mistakes; and above all, our conformity to His love, grace, mercy, and kindness. All these will come under intense scrutiny in the most difficult and trying of circumstances. It is almost as though, while we are still stargazing after the prophetic word, the Lord trips us up, throws us into a dark room, and beats the living daylights out of us! At least, that is what it feels like.

Our lives run in the opposite direction for a time as God begins to work with our character. It is here that most people let go of their vision and call. The instinctive reaction for many people, when their lives begin to run in conflicting directions to their prophecy, is to blame the prophet. It is easy to assume that because the prophet said one thing and the opposite is now occurring, then the prophecy is false. However, most accusations of false prophecy in this instance are made because of ignorance about process.

Process is a journey, a series of stages between one dimension and another. The journey is not in a straight line of upward development from the point of origin. Rather, like a bird taking off from a high point, there is a dip before there is a rise to catch the thermal under-current.

The process of God in developing our potential into something actual involves the releasing of revelation. This causes us to look up to determine our destiny, but it is followed by a decline in our fortunes as we plunge into the next stage of the process, which is confrontation.

CONFRONTATION

Revelation leads us to a point of confrontation. Literally everything within our church that would prevent God from fulfilling His Word to us will be examined. The bottom will seem like it is falling out from under the church. We will feel ourselves dropping into our own version of Joseph's pit. "Pit," as we know, is an acronym for "People In Transition."

God has never promised power without suffering. Before we receive the power of His resurrection, we must experience something of the fellowship of His sufferings. Before the release of His life, there is conformity to His death. Paul said that death works in us so that life could work in others (see 2 Cor. 4:12).

If we want to know Him in resurrection power, then we have to know Him in the fellowship of His suffering, because the two things are combined. If God has promised us life, He will give us death first, because death works life in us. We have to understand the mind of God and the ways of God. God will always deliver us to death. Paul said, "We who live are always delivered to death for Jesus' sake, that the life of Jesus also may be manifested in our mortal flesh" (2 Cor. 4:11). When Jesus was on the cross, He said, "It is finished," but He didn't ascend directly into Heaven from that point; He descended into hell. It was from hell that He went up to being seated at the right hand of the Father. Even for Jesus, that point of "It is finished" was not the end of His ordeal. What He meant was that one part was finished, but now He had another part to accomplish. He had to take back the keys and confound the enemy. He went down before He went up. He went down into hell for a purpose—to lead captivity captive, to render the enemy powerless, to take the keys of the Kingdom, and to conquer death and hell.

SPIRIT VERSUS FLESH

This part on earth was finished, but the part in the spiritual realm was not finished. So He had to go down before He could go up, and we will find that the same is true for us. There are key things that have to happen in this period of confrontation. If we do not submit to God in the confrontational period, we will not experience the transformation that needs to happen so that we can occupy what God has promised.

The next thing that will happen at some point is that all hell will break loose from inside the church. We will find that instead of climbing into a spiritual dimension, we will drop into a carnal one. We will find levels of immaturity that we did not believe could exist amongst senior Christians in our midst. We will find childishness, petulance, flesh, strife, envy, and hunger for position, as the pride and ambition of people begin to surface. As the destiny of the church begins to unfold, instead of realizing our potential for greatness, we must come to terms with our capacity for carnal behavior. He gets to work on our flesh, and instead of being elevated to a new place in the Spirit, we plunge into carnality.

Why? Because God is determined to get rid of everything in us that is rotten. We will be plunged as a church into a period of confrontation. The enemy will attack the vision and the leadership. There will be criticism and resentment. Old power struggles will reemerge and old wounds will be reopened. Anything inside us that is unresolved will come to the surface, because that is the whole point of confrontation.

We can get into the place where God wants us to be only when we actually go via the cross. God will take us right to that. He won't take us up into the heights; He will take us down into the depths. We will go into the grave and God will deal with our flesh life. The enemy will be active all around the church, but we need to know that God is going to use him to get rid of the flesh. The blessing of God may continue to fall because the Lord will not leave us comfortless.

This continued blessing is the goodness of God at work. God is simultaneous in His actions; that is, He is always doing several things at once in our lives. These actions do not have to add up together. They all can be separate and not necessarily linked in any way. We all have known God's blessing on our lives; while at the same time, the Holy Spirit convicts us of personal sin. Similarly, we have experienced the power of God corporately despite internal carnality and lack of unity.

When farmers plow their fields and then level them for planting, we see a wonderful flat surface waiting for new seed. If there is a rainfall on that field, though, the next day it will be covered in stones. The rain softens the ground, allowing what is hard within it to come to the surface. In a similar way, anything that is hard in our lives will come to the surface in this time of confrontation.

If this is happening now in the church where you are serving, take heart. God is getting rid of the flesh; the vision has not gone away and the prophecy was not wrong. God has the vision safe. It will be restored to you after the process is complete, provided that you obey and submit to Him in transition. Give Him what He wants.

In transition, we are in the process where God is making us fit the word He gave us. We may feel that we are moving further and further away from the revelation that God gave us. This is no time to look at our destiny. We must behold the process and begin to look at the character of the church.

This is not a time to dwell on projects, begin new initiatives, or commit ourselves to new ventures of faith. If we are in confrontation, it is because God is dealing with something that should not be there. Depending on where the church is in the process, we do not know how many people will leave the work during this period of testing. It is better not to plan any faith ventures involving finances until after the process is complete.

Most churches going through transition will suffer a contraction in their resources. Finances, personnel, key people in ministry, and leadership may flow out of the church initially. Some will be fair-weather friends leaving us for other pastures when the going gets tough. Generally, these people may be no significant loss. We cannot lose people who were never with us in heart in the first place. Others may be more key to our progress, and losing them will hurt us. Some will go because they may move with a job change. If things were different, they may have refused the promotion or change of work situation, but now they feel it necessary to pursue church elsewhere. Some will leave to start a new work locally and may try to take others with them.

God will always reduce us to that which is precious. Of course, for some it is the right time to go because the Lord does have other plans. Generally, though, when the heat is fierce, we are burning up that which is wood, hay, and stubble. Fire always tests our quality (see 1 Cor. 3:12-15). After the process, we may have a church that is leaner numerically, but fitter in spirit.

The gifts and the calling of God are without repentance. Let God hold on to the vision and the future; we must hold on to Him and one another.

It is the age-old battle of the Spirit against the flesh. There are some attitudes, mind-sets, and approaches that simply have to change. In confrontation, the Lord will touch our selfishness, self-preoccupation, and egotistical behavior. We all will be humbled in some way before God is satisfied that He can release us to the next level of anointing.

It seems a contradiction, but it is true, that the prophetic word about expansion should cause us to enter a period of contraction. Our first stop on the confrontation process is the cross of Jesus, followed by the grave. Death must work in our midst to God's satisfaction.

In this process, we discover that both God and the devil have their own agenda. God's agenda is life, the realization of the vision, and the entrance into a deeper anointing and a more powerful spiritual dimension. The devil's agenda is the destruction of all that we hold dear at this present time. He is wandering around us like a roaring lion seeking whom he may devour (see 1 Pet. 5:8-10).

We are encountering nothing new; we are dealing with nothing that has not been the experience of countless churches. Out of this period of suffering will come the approval of God to take us on into His plan and purpose. The enemy has three strategies in mind to use against us in this period of difficulty. These are *infiltration, depression*, and *passivity*, which, if we succumb to them, will lead us to division and decline.

INFILTRATION

The problem with confrontation is often the timing in which it occurs. No time seems to be the right time, but some are more problematic than others. It is very difficult when our church is going through this painful process of transition, whereas churches around us are enjoying a laughing anointing! We are going through our worst time ever as a church while others are basking in renewal.

The most natural thing to do at a time like this is to look for something at fault and someone to blame. If we have no revelatory rationale for current events, we will doubtless interpret them from the soul rather than from the spirit man.

Instead of looking beyond the circumstances to detect the fine hand of God at work, people look for the obvious and interpret it according to their own thinking and feeling. If the facts themselves are not obvious or do not add up totally to cover the difficulty, we invent things from our imagination, supplying pseudo-spiritual reasoning to our own particular actions.

It is always incredibly difficult to see other churches being blessed when we are under trial and testing. People would rather believe that there is a problem in the leadership; there is sin in the camp; that we have the wrong vision; or that we are out of the will of God. They want to write "Ichabod" (no glory) over the door of the church and withdraw to a more blessed place. They do not understand the purposes of God. The same process will come to every church in some way as God cleanses the temple of the church.

When something bad happens, it is easier to believe that it is the devil's work. It may well be true, but we do need the perspective of the Holy Spirit in order to see where the hand of God is moving. He allows in His wisdom what He could easily prevent by His power!

God is dealing with our flesh and our capacity to be carnal. The flesh is the only means whereby satan can get his hooks into the church. The flesh is a bigger problem to the church than any demonic intervention. The enemy tends to overplay his hand and his work becomes obvious. The flesh is much more insidious. It has many disguises and hiding places and can flare up in the most surprising of people.

Many churches are not yet good enough to be attacked by direct demonic activity. Their flesh is too good of a target to miss. Why assign a demon power to disrupt the church when pushing a few flesh buttons will have a similar effect? We do an excellent job ourselves in terms of disruption and division, when we allow the flesh-life to remain unchecked and nonaccountable.

Confrontation is the process by which God begins to work on our character and our lifestyle. Jesus said, *"The ruler of this world is coming, and he has nothing in Me"* (John 14:30).

Confrontation is designed to remove every hook of the flesh in our lives. The Lord will plunge us into crisis where every shameful thing hidden behind our public mask of spirituality will begin to surface. When the Spirit falls, the flesh will always rise. These two are ancient enemies who cannot abide each other's company.

Confrontation is the internal battle for spiritual supremacy. Will we see the carnal man crowned as the overriding power of our lives, or will the humility, gentleness, and meekness of Christ be fashioned within us as we submit to the Holy Spirit?

Will we stand and be faithful to God and people around us, or will we quit and move on, perhaps to repeat the cycle elsewhere? Of course, not all such outward/onward movements are wrong; there are many new alignments taking place in these days as the Lord repositions His people for growth.

Confrontation is God attacking the flesh. It is the work of the cross in our hearts. It is about laying down personal agendas and realizing that the Lord is killing our pride, ambition, and lack of real servanthood. He is dealing with our sin nature and our sin habit. He is breaking us; crushing us in the winepress of His dealings; chastising and scourging our carnal behavior; and getting rid of the enmity within us that casts a shadow over our relationships with Christ and His Body.

Throughout all these trials and difficulties, the Lord uses confrontation to make us fit and ready for all that He has planned. Still, many churches will not graduate to the real battlefield and remain in spiritual kindergarten because the flesh has not been laid to rest. In these instances, God has to deal with the enemy within before He can lead us to conquer the enemy on any external battleground.

In infiltration, the enemy seeks to get between people, to penetrate relationships with his poison. Marriages are a favorite target. It is hard to concentrate on spiritual developments in the church when our home-life is a battlefield of emotional hurts. Leadership teams are a choice target.

There is a simple strategy at work here—if the head is damaged, the body is made powerless. Any relationship of note and significance will come under attack in this scheme of infiltration. The devil will use ambition in people to divide and rule. He will create power struggles in key people. Unresolved issues will be encouraged to flare up again; grudges will get another opportunity to express themselves; unforgiveness will manifest itself in some pseudo-spiritual manner.

Long-standing resentments, roots of bitterness, and hidden agendas will surface at this time. The enemy will use any ego that is unbroken, any unredeemed personality or character trait to accomplish his design. All of it will be respectfully hidden under a covering, under a veneer of spirituality. These all are points of entry where the flesh cannot resist the touch of the devil. It is what the apostle Paul termed carnal behavior (see 1 Cor. 1:10-13; 3:1-9).

The more spiritual the devil can make the flesh appear, the less likely we are to understand that we have been infiltrated. In the Corinthian church, divisiveness was revealing itself in the pseudo-spiritual dialogue of the flesh playing "follow my leader" with "I am of Paul, Cephas, and Apollos," while the more astute fleshly response of "I am of Christ" captured the moral and spiritual high ground. Paul wisely cut through all this nonsense to expose carnal behavior on all sides. Carnality inhibits revelation. It keeps us in spiritual infancy where we are unable to be trusted with real truth and power.

Paul also had another apostolic perspective on this type of behavior, expressed in First Corinthians 11:17-19:

> *Now in giving these instructions I do not praise you, since you come together not for the better but for the worse. For first of all, when you come together as a church, I hear that there are divisions among you, and in part I believe it. For*

there must also be factions among you, that those who are approved may be recognized among you.

Handling the potential for division is a major part of growing up as a church. God does not create this scenario, but He does allow it to happen for a purpose.

God allows power struggles so that the church can identify who are the real leaders. In the time of conflict and power struggle, we find which leaders are really concerned about the flock and which people are more concerned about their own status and position. We discover, beneath all the spiritual rhetoric, who are preoccupied with their own vision, ministry, and anointing.

People in the church are frightened of division. They will offer any compromise between factions in order to keep things together in some semblance of unity. The issue here is not unity; it is approval. On whom is the hand of the Lord resting for focal leadership? To be able to discern correctly, examine the behavior of the people involved.

Is there someone who is being domineering, controlling, or manipulative? Is there somebody behind the scenes behaving dishonorably? Is there somebody walking around getting into every house telling stories? Is there someone on the phone to everybody causing divisions and divisiveness? Who is doing the peaceful thing, and who is doing the divisive thing? In that way, the church will know who is approved of God, because those who behave righteously in a situation are approved, while those who behave unrighteously are not. Why? Because they are grabbing for power themselves. That is where the church has to learn wisdom. Times of divisiveness are actually very important in determining who are the real "called of God" leadership in this body of people. Do not be afraid of the potential for division, just look to see how people are operating. Those who behave righteously in accordance with the fruit of the Spirit and the character of God are approved; those who are doing the opposite are clearly not, because they are walking in the flesh to get their own way.

It is part of God's way of shaping us for war so that when we get on the real battlefield, we can be confident that the person leading us has the approval and mandate of the Lord. This person really cares for our soul and will not leave us when the going gets tough. We know that we have a captain at the church and not a corporal with delusions of grandeur. Most people with some semblance of anointing can usually talk the talk, but actions under stress reveal character.

Infiltration is about the enemy gaining a point of entry to get power in the church, which will lead him to his next part of the strategy.

DEPRESSION

Continuous attack upon and within the leadership has a debilitating effect upon the soul as well as on the effectiveness of the church. Internal strife leads to a depression of faith, low morale in prayer, and dispirited worship.

The enemy wants to cause as much pain as possible so that the church will be unable to carry on in its current form. The more strife he can generate at this point, the stronger a hold he has on the church both now and in the future. Even if the issues are resolved and we stay together, he is hoping that enough damage will have occurred relationally to make the possibility of further infiltration more likely. He is quite happy for us to resolve our issues as long as there is uneasiness in our hearts toward one another and the pain of the circumstances we have endured has not been healed. This gives him ammunition for another day.

This is important to understand. We must not have resolution at any cost. To compromise now is only to store up problems for later. Christians are famous for sweeping things under the carpet. We must insist on forgiveness, inner healing, and true restoration of relationships as a prerequisite for moving forward together. The activity, program, and vision of the church must be put on hold for a season in order for full restoration to be made. Otherwise, action will dilute reconciliation. This will leave gaps for the enemy to exploit at a later date. The internal war must be fully won before the real external conflict can begin. I do not want to go into real extended conflict with the enemy if people on my side are still holding grievances.

The purpose of depression is to demoralize. It is to create as much pain, hardship, woundedness, and resentment as possible; it is to paralyze the leadership into inactivity. Depression prevents active faith by setting people against one another, so that everyone becomes weary and lethargic. Its purpose is to bring the church to a place of battle fatigue and exhaustion.

Under depression, the flesh regurgitates history. We go back over the old ground we thought had been dealt with already. The enemy digs up the cache of ammunition that he buried the last time we had an internal conflict. Unresolved issues sweep through our emotions, creating further despondency and dejection. When past history is raised, our current confusion is deepened. That is why we cannot move on from our current crisis without real forgiveness and restoration.

Where there has been a breakdown of love, trust, unity, and peace in relationships, real restoration must take place. Otherwise, we just bury our emotions for the enemy to exhume later. Any promotion of disloyalty, betrayal, and unfaithfulness must be thoroughly cleansed. All behind-the-scenes sniping and negative fellowship must be fully repented of before we can move forward, or we will simply revert to type when the pressure returns.

If we care more about what we each think, feel, and want than we do about relationships in the church, we must beware! We badly need to examine ourselves before the Lord, because we are more liable to be part of the problem than the answer.

At this point, infiltration has occurred and depression has set in, pushing us away from one another and therefore away from the purpose of God. Any cliques that form will have more potential for divisiveness than unity, even if our motives are honorable. It is simply too easy to become negative even in a wholesome way in these circumstances. All of us must be very, very careful before the Lord. Things said and done now will have repercussions for years. Godly conduct and honorable behavior will enable us to reap the blessing of God for years to come. But disreputable behavior will sow discord, continuously resulting in constant reoccurrence of internal fleshly conflict.

Even meeting together in small groups for prayer can be fraught with hidden negativity. Emotions and thoughts in times of stress demand expression. We can find ourselves talking about the issues for two hours and praying for 15 minutes.

Ironically, it is churches that have successfully negotiated these turbulent waters that have formulated core values and principles of behavior. Our God is a God of principle. His nature is unchanging, no matter what occurs. He has core values from which He operates that provide radiant confidence to all who know Him and walk with Him. He is the same yesterday, today, and forever (see Heb. 13:8). It is this unchanging nature that is part of our inheritance within the image of Christ. Core values represent the unchanging personality of God and are what we fall back on in times of relational conflict.

Debilitating depression is what occurs when we have not properly defined our core values. We therefore will react to people and situations rather than respond to the Lord. Core values enable us to focus on God and be led by the Spirit. We do not become embroiled in the carnality; rather, we allow our response to elevate us into the nature and character of God. So we practice peacemaking, love, gentleness, self-control, and kindness.

Depression causes isolation. People leave the church in search of blessing and new beginnings. The purpose of confrontation is to create a spiritual transformation within our lives, enabling us to grow up and put on the new nature. Leaving in search of blessing may seem desirable at the time, but mostly we only confirm our immaturity and inability to move up to the next level of anointing. When spiritual depression takes hold, we are ripe for the final scheme of the devil's strategy.

PASSIVITY

It is interesting to note that the people who tend to suffer the most in internal strife are the wives and children of leaders in the church. While most leaders are used to stress, conflict, and spiritual attack, it is actually their family who will come under the most direct attack. Wives in particular seem to take the brunt of relational conflict. The number of people they can talk to and confide in is at best drastically reduced if not completely destroyed. They have to be more careful than anyone else in case an unguarded word spoken in confidence is repeated by a friend who means well but acts thoughtlessly.

This is just one of the many reasons why the church must agree on an external individual or group to come and help them through the crisis. We need objectivity and a wider perspective on what God is doing. We need help to be both reconciled and restored. We need to determine our core values. External friendship and support that is impartial and anointed can enable us to emerge with credit, integrity, and destiny intact.

The team helping us through must first focus on character and the fruit of the Spirit before we get into the debate. Each of us must learn how to focus on our integrity, Christlikeness, and morality before we can realistically begin to debate the issues. What type of behavior does God expect of us in these circumstances?

Second, the team must release revelation into the church regarding the purpose of God at this time, so that we all are clear about what the Lord wants to achieve in this crisis. They must reveal the process behind the crisis so that we have a path to follow. This will alleviate many unnecessary words and feelings as we deal with them personally at the source.

Third, any outstanding grievances and judgments from a previous time must be dealt with now as a priority. We must spike the enemy ammunition and render it useless. We need a declared amnesty so that old issues can be laid to rest and not become part of the current situation.

Finally, the team must be allowed to arbitrate the issues to a meaningful and long-lasting settlement, at the heart of which is genuine reconciliation of relationships and restoration of vision and purpose. It is important that this external team has the broad support of the majority of the people and that they are truly capable of being objective and impartial. This is not Christian gangsterism where we get our friends in to get others to toe the line!

Without that external frame of reference, we will slide quickly into depression and passivity. If the crisis goes on too long without resolution, some will give up. A malaise will set in that hinders prayer and productivity. Some will cease trying to participate. Lateness or nonattendance in meetings will become prevalent. There will be no spark in worship because emotions are at a low ebb. Some will be hoping that a word of faith may penetrate the fog of their uncertainty. We will have lost our ability to generate faith from within our own spirit. We will become tired and dispirited, too weary even to continue talking over the same ground. We will have no energy. Everything will be a trial and a pain. We will sadly conclude that it is better for us to leave. We may search for spiritual reasons regarding why we are jumping ship— more to make ourselves feel better than to validate our actions. Some will simply fold their tents and steal away.

Our ability to focus on anything significant will be much reduced. We will feel isolated and unsure of who we can properly relate to in the church. There will be a loss of faith and initiative. Subversion and passivity will become the order of the day. Faithfulness will be discontinued by some people, particularly in the area of personal help and financial support. Key workers will lose their drive and take sabbaticals. Financial input will drop as people withhold their substance until the situation stabilizes. Unfortunately, many of these people do not store up their tithes and offerings; they just stop giving!

Some will begin to choose sides in the issue or try to stay neutral. We will choose sides often on the basis of friendship rather than obedience to God or any outward signs of righteousness and morality. We will not consider that it is possible for people to be right about the issue but morally corrupt in their behavior and how they handle the situation. I have known men to be very accurate about the issues but use the situation to feed their own selfish desires and ambition. I also have known people who have been wrong about the issue but morally circumspect in how they handled the situation. Character under stress is more valuable than an accurate diagnosis. In situations containing great potential for unrighteous behavior, always mark the people who behave like Jesus.

Passivity is destructive and will lead to division and a continuance of improper behavior, resulting in ongoing strife within the village, town, city, or region.

DETERMINE THE ORIGIN OF FOUNDATIONS

Even some people who left the church early on in the dispute will still snipe at people from the cowardly safety of noninvolvement. They represent a fifth column still at work within the body perpetuating the infiltration, depression, and ongoing passivity that the enemy so loves. Some who left will still want their influence to be felt in the work. They will not be under authority anymore, but they will still persist in sowing their perspective—however relevant or poisonous it may be—into the homes of people who have chosen to stay.

This type of activity could probably fall into the category of manipulation, control, and domination. If we have left, we must abandon our place in the issue. We have no voice now and must render our part in the issue inactive. If we are sought out, we must express no opinion. It is important to be scrupulously correct in our thinking, speaking, and behaving. We can pray blessing on people but must not give advice. If we have taken ourselves out, we must stay out! The wrath of God at this type of behavior will eventually catch up with us later as we reap whatever we sow.

I have known many churches to begin operation in times like this and suffer the exact same reversal. When churches are going through internal strife, it is my practice to determine the source of their beginning. How did they originate? In my limited experience, I have discovered that approximately 70 percent of churches going through internal warfare were actually birthed in similar circumstances. A number of these churches are going through legitimate transition because God has a purpose to elevate them to a new place of anointing and vision.

Other churches, however, are simply reaping what they have sown from their point of origin. If God does not own the getting of something, He cannot own the having of it! How we start dictates how we finish. Churches that began in rebellion will end in ignominy. We must determine the reason for our current distress in the church and not just assume we are in transition to a more powerful place.

It may be that our history has caught up with us, and we must determine now what the Lord would have us do. Is He allowing us a period of chastisement where we are being humbled to seek repentance and forgiveness from those we have wronged? Is He scourging us of our arrogance and ambition? Must we make an act of public repentance and contrition in order to set right the past and bring healing and reconciliation? If so, we need to appoint an external team to help us fully obey the process of repentance.

However, it simply may be that the Lord never intended our church to start. He was never in the split and does not endorse our activity. We may have blessed people individually (because God is faithful to us personally), but we have never been able to grow corporately to any level of significance. Our corporate vision has never taken off; we have found ourselves stumbling from one good idea to another, but nothing has really worked. We have a modicum of success but no sustainable breakthrough. People join and people leave, but spiritually we are not really going anywhere. Our church may have a history of continuous divisiveness and splitting. That may tell us something if we have the heart to listen. We may well be wasting our life and our substance on something that will never grow from personal blessing into corporate anointing.

In crisis, we must evaluate our history in an attitude of openness and honesty. We can fool ourselves and deceive other people, but God is not mocked. What we sow, we will reap. Some churches need to close their doors and disband. Whatever spirit of division and rebellion that we have entertained and given room to, must be driven out of the area. We must apologize to other churches. Our people must be delivered of rebellion and deception before being placed honorably with other churches. Any revenue from the sale of property and equipment plus the current account can be given to missions or sowed into the unity of the churches in the area. What began in dishonor can be terminated in full righteousness, giving no place to the enemy.

Our demise must be honorable, or we sow continuous problems into other churches through the conduct of the people we have given away. Receiving churches must be kind and merciful but firm enough in relationship to ensure that past behavior does not remain current practice.

Confrontation is the touch of God against the flesh. It is the hand of God moving unseen behind the enemy and sinful man, orchestrating the downfall of everything that would prevent Him from achieving His dream for the Church. The Lord uses everything to destroy the work of the world, the flesh, and devil in our midst. However, it is not all gloom and doom. In the midst of the desperate process of change, we will see Christ walking among us spreading His fragrance and beauty in our hearts. Heaven will come to earth as the Holy Spirit broods over our seeming chaos, affecting a transforming work in our lives. We will suffer the loss of many things, but we will gain the one thing that makes it all worthwhile—the love of Jesus...the beauty of His presence manifested among us.

TRANSFORMATION

Through the violence of the confrontational issues surrounding us, God does a work of transformation. In the stormy process of Spirit versus flesh, He removes our old nature and soaks us in the new nature of Christ.

Jesus is established in our hearts as we develop the fruit of His character. The fruit of the Spirit always grows best in poor soil. When others are being unkind, the gentle nature of Christ is formed in us as we respond in kindness in return. Faithfulness grows in situations where we are tempted to walk away but choose to be loyal and stay. Peace is established within as we choose to stay and rest in the midst of the turmoil and the tumult of adversity. It is called moving in the opposite spirit to what is coming against our life. It is loving our enemies, praying for those who use us, and blessing our persecutors. As we submit to the will of God, we learn obedience through our suffering and deliver ourselves to a place where God can trust us. He trusts what we manifest of His Son.

This process does not have to be completely pain-filled and desperate. The joy of the Lord is our strength (see Neh. 8:10). For the joy set before us, we can endure this divine treatment of the cross in our lives. As we learn to humble ourselves, the Father will joyfully fill us with a greater presence of His Son. As the manifestation of Christ's presence increases, so does the fruit of the Spirit, which is the nature of God. Our pleasure in God increases and we are filled with joy, encouragement, and comfort of the Spirit. Our desire for the Lord increases with our submission, turning to delight in our daily lives.

Confrontation/transformation is a combined process engineered by God to kill off our flesh and enliven us in His Spirit. Unless we allow ourselves to submit to the Lord, we can never fully inherit the totality of our prophetic call. The process worked in Joseph but failed in Saul, whereas David's life appears to be a cycle of contradiction that constantly brought him into confrontation with God and transformation within. God eventually regretted making Saul king because it seemed that he could never grasp the significance of the process the Lord was using to change him. David, though frail and imperfect on many occasions, actually learned enough in the turbulence of his life for God to call him *"a man after My own heart"* (Acts 13:22b).

When Israel came out of Egypt, the shortest route to Canaan was through Philistine territory. Though Israel was armed for battle, the Lord took the people the long way round because they were not ready for the fight (see Exod. 13:17).

There are shortcuts in the Spirit, but you have to be of a certain caliber and quality to endure the fight that you will find on that journey. It is not easy! There is a particular tempering that is required. The desert route was God's way of changing weaklings into warriors.

The Church is looking for acts of power to provide a shortcut into a new dimension of life, love, and service. However, every move of God delivers us to the cross of Christ, from which there is no escape. The move of God within us creates a willingness to take up the Cross, die daily, and follow Jesus. The cross understands the process of death to life that the Lord is establishing in our lives.

In the process of transformation, God has three strategies to combat the schemes of the devil and to establish His own will in the Church. It is confrontation for a season to provide transformation for a reason. In order to occupy the high territory of the Spirit that is our inheritance, we must conform to the image of Christ and become supernatural as Christ is formed within.

We can learn to enjoy this work of God as well as endure it. Jesus, for the joy that was set before Him, endured the Cross (see Heb. 12:2). This also must become our response in this direct work of the cross. God is nailing things in our lives that simply must die. It pleased God to bruise Jesus, and it pleases God to bruise us also. It is supposed to be painful. However, in transformation, we also will know incredible love and comfort as God soothes our pain and ministers to us in our distress. In the Garden of Gethsemane, an angel ministered to Jesus as He prayed to be wholehearted in the will of God, knowing the suffering that would entail (see Luke 22:42-43). God is bringing us to a place where He can actually trust us with the very thing that He prophesied over us in the first place. He is doing a work of transformation.

He is purifying the temple, cleaning His house. He is pruning us, cutting us back that we might become more fruitful. We can consciously work toward His goal or unconsciously oppose it. If we cooperate, it is a short, sharp, intense, and very painful death. If we resist or fail to flow with the process of change, we unwittingly make the whole thing longer than perhaps necessary.

Out of every ten churches that have entered transition, approximately half have not made it. The flesh was too strong. The church went from revelation into confrontation, but then the church split and went back to revelation. I have seen a number of churches with a revelatory word about moving from being a good local church to being a resource church of an Antioch nature. Some of these churches are now broken and very probably will never rise to that high calling. They could not endure the contradiction.

In the violence of the confrontation and transformation process, they could not stay on the cross. It hurt too much. The reason that confrontation and transformation are combined into one process is because God wants us to behold Jesus. He wants us to hold on to Him and be held by Him. We do not enter and endure contradiction and then pass through transformation. If they followed after each other, none of us would make it. They are a combined work of God. The devil is loose, but Jesus is present! The flesh is dying, but the new nature is rising. We are losing our friends in the natural but growing in friendship with God in the Spirit. We are shedding our old wineskin and forming a new one.

The first of God's three strategies is communion with Him.

COMMUNION WITH GOD

God wants to be present as we transition, but how do we enter into communion with God? The first thing we have to do is humble ourselves before God. If we humble ourselves, He will exalt us in due time. However, if we exalt ourselves by not giving in to the process, it will be harder for us later on. I can remember teaching on this subject in a particular place in America. I was there for a week, and I taught on transition for the first couple of days. One night, as I arrived early at the church before the meeting, there was a particular guy with a group of people in the church building, commenting on this teaching of the whole death process. He was remarking that he considered the process to be foolish, questioning how could we enjoy this whole thing if God was leading us to death. He was going to move on elsewhere and enjoy life!

That was his attitude: "I am not staying around here to get kicked around by this, that, and the other; you have got to kiss your brains good-bye to actually live in this whole thing." Then he noticed me standing at the doorway and he said, "No offense, preacher." I said, "None taken, and I quite understand your point of view. But I want to say to you, it pretty much doesn't matter where you go; the process is going to follow you. You can do it either here right now or wherever you go next. The next church is probably in the same thing too, either by the time you get there or after the first few months of your being there. The more you keep running away, the more difficult you are going to make it for yourself. God is going to get more and more difficult with you. Jesus put it this way: You can either stumble over this rock and be broken, or this rock can fall on you and you will be crushed. Now your attitude is, 'I am not stupid. I am not staying around to endure all this pain. I am off.' That is fine. My attitude is, 'I know that I can't avoid this thing. I would rather be broken than crushed, but I cannot avoid being hit. I want to stumble over this thing and be broken. I do not want something to fall on me from a great height and crush me.' You pay your money and make your choice, and my choice is to stay here and die right now. Hey, you live your life the way you want to, Pal."

I want to be more conscious of the glory of change in transformation than I am of the pain of change in confrontation. I want communion with God, so I am prepared to humble myself so that I can please Him with all my responses. On the days when I have to grit my teeth, cry my tears, and endure, I want to hold on to Him as He holds on to me. On the days when I can smile because the pain is just a dull ache, I want to resolve to continue with God in the process.

> *My brethren, take the prophets, who spoke in the name of the Lord, as an example of suffering and patience. Indeed we count them blessed who endure. You have heard of the perseverance of Job and seen the end intended by the Lord—that the Lord is very compassionate and merciful* (James 5:10-11).

If we really are going to rise to a place where our own personal anointing and faith level is high, then we will need to know what real communion with God is. All ministry comes out of relationship. Power comes out of suffering, and anointing comes out of intimacy. It is in communion with God that we learn how to humble ourselves under His hand. There is no point in complaining. The most positive thing we can do in confrontation is to fast and humble ourselves before God. We then ask the Lord to let His light shine into our lives. Is there anything in our life that He would not be happy with?

In that process of building communion, we learn how to live in the character of Jesus. We learn how to make the first commandment first: *"Love the Lord your God with all your heart, with all your soul, with all your mind, and with all your strength"* (Mark 12:30a). It is in that time of communion that the fruit of the Spirit is established. It is always interesting to me that in a time of confrontation, people talk about gifts and power when they should talk about fruit and character. That is what confrontation is about. It is always about fruit and character, about the life of Jesus, not the power of Jesus. It is always about the life of Jesus, not the work of Jesus.

When we are in confrontation, when we are under pressure, God is talking to us about fruit and character.

In communion, the Lord works a new level of intimacy into our lives. Standing still under the hand of God, wanting His will to be fulfilled no matter what cost to ourselves, is one of the most intimate responses we can make to Him. Kneeling down to kiss the hand that hurts creates an intimacy that truly glorifies the Lord.

When we choose to submit to the Lord in times of great adversity, it is because our hearts are crying out for intimacy and communion. Part of that closeness is a new level of prayer that arises out of a broken and contrite heart. We give God permission to touch anything in our lives, and we ask for His faithfulness to endure so that His will may be done.

In communion, our behavior before God is moving us into godliness and righteousness. The character of Jesus becomes our prominent desire—to be transformed into the image of Jesus. There is a constant presentation of ourselves before the Lord. We live in the edict of Romans 12:1-2:

> *I beseech you therefore, brethren, by the mercies of God, that you present your bodies a living sacrifice, holy, acceptable to God, which is your reasonable service. And do not be conformed to this world, but be transformed by the renewing of your mind, that you may prove what is that good and acceptable and perfect will of God.*

Every day we receive His mercy, presenting ourselves to Him and asking for renewal of mind so that transformation can take place. As the pain and difficulty of confrontation abounds, so does the presence of God in transformation. Our minds are assailed by the adversity of our circumstances, but as we present ourselves humbly before His mercy, His thinking renews our mind. We live through one more day proving the will of God in transition. In communion, we learn to live in day-tight compartments before Him. As we present ourselves at the beginning of a new day, we gradually begin to experience the newness of life that God re-creates within. New every morning is His mercy and His steadfast love (see Lam. 3:21-26).

As we grow in our personal communion with the Lord, then He becomes the central issue in the transition process. We are turned around from dwelling on the pain and loss to begin to understand and experience the gain of transformation. The presence of God begins to increase upon us. Worship begins to blossom and reach for new heights. Every church should write songs that signify the love of God in the time of trial. Every church should keep a journal that details the prophecies, vision statement, and mission of the church that makes up our corporate revelation and destiny. Added to that should be a record of God's dealings with the church in the transition process.

Unity should become an issue in our hearts. We need to unite around our love for Jesus and ask the Holy Spirit to enable us to find new ways of loving and caring for one another. This will lead us into the second part of God's strategy.

COVENANT TO THE HOUSE

The church is the dwelling place of God by the Spirit. He lives in our relationships, not in our meetings. It is the love or lack of it between God's people that attracts Him to us or denies Him access.

We are living stones being fitted together with others to provide a home for God in our friendships (see 1 Pet. 2:4-8; Eph. 2:19-22).

The confrontation/transformation process has been designed by the Lord to increase the degree of fit between God's people. Transition shapes and dresses our life so that we can successfully take our place alongside others. Transition squares us up and gets rid of all our rough edges, which prevent real unity from happening.

The process destroys carnality and independence, and allows God's love to cement us together in a new bonding of love and friendship. It is so important to the Lord that we redefine our covenant together as people brought together to serve the purposes of God. Out of transition should come a new set of core values—principles of loving relationship that we can fall back on in times of adversity, so that we never again fall prey to friction and divisiveness.

Redefining our covenant walk together and reestablishing our core values are vital parts of coming out of transition into a new place before God as a church. In transition, the whole church (or as many as remain!) needs to discuss together the issues of friendship and loving relationship.

We must, with great deliberation, think through what we want from our relationships and make covenant at a new level. Wherever our hearts are joined together with others, we must strengthen the ties that bind us together. Friends must talk openly of their love for one another and their desire for a stronger heart connection. Existing relationships must become more inclusive as we open our circle to involve fresh people. No one should be lonely. Those who are loners must be loved into submitting that side of their nature in order to evolve a relational lifestyle. We cannot change people's personalities. Some people are naturally more open and gregarious. However, we all have to make relational adjustments in order to build a habitation for the Lord.

Covenant must be redefined around openness and honesty; non-negotiable love in times of adversity; believing the best of one another; making negative fellowship and criticism an offense against the house; looking out for one another; and considering others more important. If we looked through a concordance for all the "one another" verses and practiced them, church would be a radically different place. Do everything to make God welcome!

Redefine the servant-spirit heart of the church; talk about love and unity, sacrifice, mutual trust, and obedience to God on a corporate level. Come to the place of the early Church, who were of one mind, one heart, one accord, and all together.

Make sure that the presence of God is your priority, not just His power. God is present when covenant is made and kept. He will test our covenant, so be prepared for that. We want to build a church that is so attractive to God that He cannot stay away.

This kind of covenant can be forged only in the adversity of transition. We can design covenant at any time, but it can be made real only in adversity. It has to be tested. In adversity, real communion and covenant are forged in the house of the Lord. Testing makes it or breaks it. We must make sure that our relationships are strong enough to attract the presence of God as well as to endure the warfare that our corporate anointing will provoke.

We all will be under attack in this new dimension. That is part of the adventure and the excitement of walking in a new place with God. We get to see a whole new level of His majesty and supremacy. We must learn how to stand together and fight for one another (as opposed to against each other!). In covenant, we send out a message to the enemy: "If you attack one of us, you attack all of us. If you trouble one household, we all will come after you! Everything you do against us will only drive us closer to God and one another. We will not be infiltrated anymore. We will deal with the enemy within. You will have no place among us."

Jonathan did not make a covenant with David when everything was going well. He made it when his own father was seeking to kill his friend. It was forged in adversity. Jesus said to His disciples, *"You are those who have continued with Me in My trials"* (Luke 22:28). Their relationship was developed within the warfare generated by Jesus' ministry.

Difficult times are the making of a church if we can hold together. If our difficulties drive us apart, it is probably because we did not have much in the way of relationship and friendship. Real covenant is defined in times of danger, difficulty, and diversity.

It is an unwritten law in relationships that all friendships will be tested. We have to know who are our real friends. Which friendship is only at a surface level? Which relationships are based around performance? If I am doing well and am successful, people flock around me, but if the wheels come off my wagon, do I have any real friends—those who will ride the storm with me?

We mostly make covenants or expressions of love and friendship in good times when all is well. Relational storms signify if our hearts are true.

That is why God is dealing with the enemy within, dealing with our carnality, so that He can raise us to that level where we make covenant and live it out with each other. When the church is going through profound distress because God is sorting people out on the inside, the one thing that He will want to establish in that particular church is covenant. That is what our present distress is all about—it is about us personally coming into greater communion with God and collectively coming in to covenant in the house of God. He will want to establish covenant in the time of distress. The enemy wants to split us apart, infiltrate, demoralize, subvert our relationships, divide, rule, and close down the church. God is looking for us all to come together, start standing together, and make a new covenant to the house of God.

In distress, we must redefine covenant in our midst. Don't wait until everything is going well; start looking at it right now. What is the process of covenant? Don't wait until things get better, because we could be hopelessly divided by then. The only way we move forward in this time of distress and attack the enemy is by making covenant with each other. We choose to believe the best about each other, choose to stand together, choose to understand that this whole thing is the work of the Cross and nothing more, and that we must allow God to deal with our hearts. Reestablishing the core values of God will become a matter of policy in our friendships.

One of our major core values must be that we love each other no matter what is happening. Another is that in times of tension and difficulty, our love is nonnegotiable. So if we are having differences in the leadership, our love is never on the negotiating table. We love each other no matter what, and we stay together. We are just having a difference of opinion, but we are committed 100 percent to each other. Loving each other is a core value and principle.

We live together in relationships that are based on God's principles, not a worldly value system. The world values success, wealth, position, status, good looks, and charisma. If those elements diminish in the world, friendship can fluctuate accordingly.

God loves us according to His principled nature. He is unchanging in the way that He acts toward us. The loving-kindness of God is from everlasting to everlasting. It is fresh every morning. He forgives and He forgets. He is gracious and kind, slow to anger, swift to bless. His goodness and kindness enable us to apologize and be changed. He is the same yesterday, today, and forever (see Heb. 13:8). Grace is a core value with our heavenly Father. In our sinfulness and stupidity, His love is unchanging. He practices the fruit of the Spirit in our lives! This is how God treats us in good times and in bad; when we are doing well or poorly. How can we be any different from Him?

In times of demoralization and stress, we must redefine our core values, for they are what we will hold onto while going through the storm. They are what will stop us from sinking into depravity and sin; they will prevent us from dividing and splitting off, breaking our covenant to the house of God. We are building relationships of mutual trust and honesty, of openness and obedience to God, of integrity, of love and unity, having a fervent spirit toward one another.

We are living in sacrifice and being committed to each other. We are speaking those values out, living them out, and working them out in the violence of the situation that we are caught up in.

In distress, as a church, we will discover who is really joined to us in heart and who is joined to the euphoria of what was happening in the meetings.

When churches are expanded in the Spirit realm, they have an influx, an increase of people joining. Everyone wants to be where the anointing is present. I would counsel churches not to make big plans for new buildings and expenditure too soon. Do not get carried away by the momentum of current success.

Every time of expansion is followed by a period of contraction. Wait till the storm hits. Then see who remain faithful when God is pruning the work. It is a scriptural principle that after a time of heavy fruit, pruning must occur in order to increase our potential for future success.

See who remains after pruning has taken place. These are your real disciples; anyone else was just a hanger-on. In times of blessing, all the spiritual nomads come out of the woodwork. In adversity, they will disappear. This is what we call "felt-led" poisoning. During times of blessing, people "feel led" to join us; during adversity, they "feel led" to go elsewhere. Such people are rootless and will never grow. They are clouds without rain. They have a form of godliness but no power. No root means no fruit. We simply cannot count on them. Of course, we are not denying the power of God to change such people. However, we do not start counting Christians until the storm is over! These people do not have any concept of sacrifice or faithfulness. They keep drinking out of someone else's well instead of digging their own.

It is in times of difficulty when we learn what covenant is really all about. If all we are doing when the going gets tough is going somewhere else, we will never actually put down roots. I remember a guy coming up to me at a conference and asking, "Will you pray for me? I need a prophetic word over my life." I lifted my heart to the Lord and the Lord said to me: "Don't you dare prophesy over him!" So I said to the Lord, "Okay, fine. Would You mind telling me why?" He answered, "Son, this guy has been a nomad for ten years.

"The problem in his life is that he has got no root system, because he never stays in a place long enough. He wants you to bless him. If you pray for him, Graham, I will bless him because you are praying for him. However, you will not be helping him because all you will do is bless him in his disobedience. He needs to stop wandering. He needs to stop this spiritual fornication that he is involved in, staying in one place only when things are good and then leaving and not taking any responsibility. He needs to stop that nomadic way of life and put down roots. The real problem with him is that he has no root system. Even what you bless him with, he cannot sustain and keep or hold. He will lose it because he has no roots."

I looked at this guy and I said, "Well, God has told me that I can't prophesy over you because you are a nomad. You haven't got any roots, and your real problem is that you keep going from church to church and you have no root system. Therefore, you are never going to hold onto any blessing that God gives you. So until the time comes when you obey the Lord, put down roots, work through all the problems that you have in your own life, and stop projecting things onto other people, you will never actually know the sustained blessing of God in your life, and you will always be rootless. When the wind of adversity comes, you will be the first one blown out. I will not prophesy over you, but with your permission, I will pray that you will put down roots and learn faithfulness to God and His people." He merely said something extremely unpleasant and left.

COMMITMENT TO THE LEADERSHIP

Generally, we get the leaders we pray for—or not, as the case may be. In transition, the leaders are going to be particularly vulnerable. They will be the main target of demonic attack from outside and fleshly connivance from inside the church. They need love, support, and prayer at this time. Instead, they will usually receive criticism, complaints, and accusations. They will come under attack in all kinds of insidious ways.

Internally, some people may make a power play by seeking to undermine their leadership, authority, and gifting. This will usually come from within the leadership, from a particular ministry within the church, or from someone who feels that his gifting and ministry has not been promoted in the way he would like. Then there are the vultures from other churches—leaders and ministries who feed off these types of situations. On the surface, they offer a shoulder for our people to cry on—tea and sympathy with prayer and "prophetic counsel." It appears benevolent but belies the grasping power underneath. They will deny sheep stealing and simply say they are growing better grass. A thief is a thief.

Most of this activity goes on in private and secret. I believe that we should be cautious about people joining us from other churches in the locality. We do not want to deny people the right to move on in the purpose of God; however, we must make sure that it is the purpose of God. Don't steal sheep. Birth some new ones out of the world. Transfer growth seldom works effectively. It can take years to work some things through with people unless we have a move of God upon them. Better to have fresh fish than someone else's kippers.

Of course, I do realize that many people have been smoked by the ungodly fires of some leaders and ministries. I do not want to deny people a place of healing. However, they must be willing to eventually get healed, delivered, and move on in the purpose of God.

In transition, there is a spirit of accusation that is dispatched to attack the leadership. Again, we must fall back on our core values in this type of situation. Most leaders will not have trod this path before, so mistakes will happen. Mistakes that arise out of ignorance and inadequacy are par for the course, entirely understandable, and easily forgiven.

Defend your leaders against the flesh and the demonic. Guard their back. We do not have to become "yes men" who live in perpetual agreement with leadership. We are allowed to have private disagreements as long as our love and commitment are not on the negotiating table if things do not work out how we want. Disagree by all means, but remain faithful to the core values of God.

Pray for your leaders. If you are having it tough, they are probably having a harder time. One of the reasons churches split is because people stop praying for their leaders in the distress that they are experiencing. Leaders are vulnerable and human and need the protection and shield of our love and prayers.

Transition is a time when we should express our commitment to leaders and act it out. They need to know who they can count on in the battle that is raging. If we withdraw in seasons of trouble, we will never gain strength as a church to attack the enemy. Write a letter, send a gift, take them for a meal, and pray for their home and family. Stand with them publicly.

They will not be right about everything. That clearly would be an unrealistic expectation. They are under immense pressure and will inevitably not see some things as they should, yet the grace of God can cover our mistakes as we go through transition. The valley is no place for making decisions. Let us try and leave, when possible, major decisions until we regain our equilibrium.

Transition is a character issue. As our leaders take hits in transition, they will need a prayer shield. They will need friends whom they can confide in, people who will knock out the dents in their armor, and they will need continual expressions of love before this thing is over. The violence of transition may last for months, and their confidence may become fragile despite outward appearances. The buildup of pressure will be huge, and leaders will need somewhere to vent just as we all do.

We don't have to get creepy on people and fawn all over them. Neither is this an opportunity to insinuate ourselves into any future power base. It is love for the sake of love. It is representing God's heart and capacity to bless, restore, and support.

In times of continuous stress, our leaders will need the Aarons and the Hur to hold up their arms just as they did for Moses in the fight against a resourceful enemy (see Exod. 17:8-13). Leaders need to know that God is protecting them and that people are believing the best and praying over their lives.

Commitment to the leadership now in transition will enable us to develop the authority for future warfare as we take ground. In transition, we are defending the ground that we possess, but we also are developing the authority to increase our territory in the future. Something is forged in transition between leaders and the church.

This is where God learns whether He can trust us and thrust us into the real battle for supremacy in the region. Stand together in faithfulness. Be faithful to the Lord, the vision, the house, and the leadership. The enemy will try and make you passive in your response to leaders. Be active in expression. Be visible in serving. Make it a joy for leaders to be over the church. Let your yes be a yes verbally! Expression deepens impression.

Our ability to hold together during transition will strengthen our corporate character, causing a greater flow of sanctification and godliness. This is where we will begin to rule as we earn a place of trust with Almighty God.

RECEIVE EXTERNAL HELP

In transition, we will need friends from outside who can provide objective support and care. We also need access to people who understand transition and process. In transition, we are re-digging the foundations of the church so that the Lord can erect a bigger building and release a greater dynamic of corporate power and identity. The only people who can really help us now are apostles and prophets, the foundation ministries.

It is inevitable in transition that our structures are going to change. New paradigms need to form as God delivers us from being a stereotype to a prototype church. Changes must come. We need prophetic insight and apostolic strategy combining together to redevelop the foundation and structure of the work.

We will need external help to cultivate our core values and to redefine our friendships. We must suspend as much as we are able of our program in favor of meetings that will build, support, and sustain us through the process of change, for a season. The quality of relationships must improve or our corporate character will be diminished. Unity must be practiced. Trust must go to a deeper level.

We need these external ministries to enable us to work through our differences. It is not just on the public platform that we need building ministries, though. It is also needed in our discussions at leadership level. The new wineskin needs to be described by prophetic input from a building prophet. There are blessing prophets who are good in public meetings, speaking and prophesying over people. Only a building prophet can speak of the future in the violence of transition and inspire people to hold on together. A building prophet will make himself available to counsel, advise, and continuously inspire the church in this difficult period.

Apostles and prophets together are the eye in the storm, bringing peace and order into chaos. They are a catalyst to provide breakthrough. Through teaching, advice, prophecy, and impartation, they can furnish the building blocks to enable us to bridge the gap between where we are now and where we aspire to be.

MANIFESTATION

The combined resources of apostle and prophet will bring us to the place in God where there is a release in the Spirit realm.

In transition, our corporate identity will be released and a new life message will form. Manifestation is the fulfillment and the revealing of all that God declared to us in revelation at the onset of the process. The Lord now trusts us enough to cause us to rise up and occupy a new place.

Transformation has worked and our character has grown before God, giving Him confidence in our capacity to live at this new level. He gave us the original word, then plunged us into confrontation and transformation to enable our character to rise to a place where that word could be released. Now we fit the word that we have received, and a whole new realm of power and anointing will open up to us.

We cannot merely pray down the presence of God; we must attract Him by the quality of our relationships. We must become living stones fitted together into a house of God. The Lord is not looking for great meetings. He is looking for a house. If we build it, He will come!

Through transformation we are made beautiful before the Lord. He becomes attracted to our holiness and love for one another. There is a blessing in unity that attracts the Holy Spirit. There is a curse in dis-unity that attracts the demonic. Worship begins to grow in our midst because we are falling more in love with Jesus. Our corporate identi-ty and vision are reestablished in our midst, and we inherit a season of divine acceleration. A quickening spirit is released that speeds up the new spiritual growth we need, to occupy this new place. Time that we thought would be lost and wasted in transition is now mysterious-ly made up as God commits Himself to manifestation in our midst. People begin to grow and accelerate in the Spirit.

Faith begins to be magnified in people's hearts as they hear the Lord in a fresh way. We come to that place in our occupation where souls begin to fall into the Kingdom. There is an anointing upon indi-viduals to witness; there is an anointing on the church to reap the harvest that God is actually giving us. We will find that all the people round about us, who God has been preparing, unbeknownst to us, suddenly start coming to the church and finding the Lord.

God starts digging us wells on housing developments where we never had a presence. He gives us property in places where we never actually thought of moving to. All sorts of things begin to happen around us. God begins to give us our inheritance—and the land along with it. He enlarges our boundaries in the natural as well as in the spiritual. Suddenly, our territory increases because, in confrontation, God has transformed us and now is trusting us, actually marking out our inheritance and territory. God is the original territorial spirit; the enemy is just a copy. He said to Israel, "I will mark your territory from the Euphrates River down to the sea," and He gave them the boundaries (see Deut. 11:24). That is a territorial spirit at work.

The devil has never done anything original. All he does is copy God. God is a territorial spirit, so the devil wants to be one as well. God will give us our inheritance, and we will find our territory will begin to increase. Everything we come into now will come to us through the warfare of transition. Don't be frightened of this whole process, which God loves; He knows the place it will lead us to. He will walk us through it hand in hand. During time, we will discover God in ways that we never thought we would ever know Him.

I have worked with churches in transition for a number of years, and I love the whole process. I find it remarkable. It is fascinating to help churches begin to see God in a way they never understood Him before. They begin to experience God and come to a place where they realize that nothing can hurt them. Nothing can touch them. This is where their anointing in warfare and battle really gets birthed in their hearts.

We begin learning about what it is to rely on the presence of God and on the person of God. When He comes, He comes in power and in faith, and everything comes with Him. And when we make space for the King of kings, His presence with us gives incredible heart and faith to enable us to press through transition. Even the whispers of God will cause great faith to rise. But before we become a church that moves in the manifest presence of God, we first have to be conformed to His image—and that happens only through confrontation.

The prophecy and vision we received in revelation now begin to unfold. Divine appointments begin to happen. God is in the house and in control!

THE LAW OF RETRIBUTION

In the violence of confrontation, there will be some people who will leave us. Some will be fair-weather friends and perhaps no great loss. Others may be leaders and ministries—key people in the work in spiritual, financial, and relational terms. We may lose friends and people whom we have come to depend on. All our resources will come under attack.

Whatever the prophetic promises about resources and anointing that God will release to us, we will suffer a contraction before we experience expansion. It is a grievous experience when we know that people who should have known better, leave us and go elsewhere—people who have a level of maturity and wisdom but cannot see the point of what is happening. Some leave because of personal ambition. Others leave for a quieter life and greener pastures. People who we thought were anchor points are now no longer there, and we feel adrift in a sea of turmoil.

Surprising things happen in transition. Anchor people leave, and those who were drifting suddenly put down roots and are a stabilizing influence. Adversity changes people for the better as well as the worst. The devil steals people away from the work, but not everyone who leaves is deceived. Some leave legitimately in God. Many, though, are taken from us, and we cannot endorse their departure.

In manifestation, the Lord makes the enemy pay for his handiwork. In Exodus 22:1, we read, *"If a man steals an ox or a sheep, and slaughters it or sells it, he shall restore five oxen for an ox and four sheep for a sheep."*

An ox is a working animal and therefore represents a leader or a key gift in the church. A sheep represents a church member. I believe we have permission at this time to ask for retribution and repayment. Look back over the period of transition to people who have been lost to us. Possibly, we had to release an "enforced" church plant because a bunch of people were set on leaving and that was the most positive way to do it.

Count up all the key workers and church people who were lost. Name the types of ministries that were stripped away from the church. For every gifted person and leader, we want five caliber replacements. For every church member lost, we want four new people.

This is important! To really pay the enemy back, we must ask the Lord for replacements at the new level we are occupying. We do not want replacement people at the old pre-transition level. We want people who can be a resource now at this new level. We are asking for an increase of people with the capacity to inherit and minister in the new land of occupation. We need to make the enemy regret all that he has done against us!

We must come together before the Lord in the manner of the widow in Luke 18:1-8, who constantly came to the judge for justice. After being refused many times, the widow finally received justice from him because of her persistence. Note that her cry was, *"Avenge me of mine adversary!"* (KJV).

God is the exact opposite of this unrighteous judge. He is not unwilling to hear us. However, we need to come before Him with persistence to request that He judges the enemy on our behalf. We must ask for a restoration of new people at a new level. We must ask for retribution according to Exodus 22:1.

We want people who fit the new paradigm. We want resource church people who will fit us now and add immediate weight to current spiritual developments. Ask and keep on asking.

Some of these people will join us from elsewhere. Others will suddenly accelerate growth from within. Do not stop praying until these people are present. Enjoy this time in particular. This is our opportunity to proclaim the favor of the Lord and vengeance on the enemy (see Isa. 61:2). Have fun getting revenge on the devil—make him pay. Above all, enjoy this new place in the Spirit. Learn to bask in the warmth of God's favor and blessing. This is a new day!

Section Five

THIRD-DAY PREACHING

Chapter Twelve

REDEPLOYING THE PREACHER

WHILE I would never denigrate the necessity for the kerygma, the Good News to be declared, Romans 10:14 still standing as a necessity, ("...*how shall they hear without a preacher?*"), I can't stop asking the question as to whether it is possible that, as the gap widens between the talkers and the listeners, we simultaneously lessen people's eagerness and effectiveness in being message carriers to their own world? By turning our professional pulpits into the "Olympics of Oratory," do we, in fact, continue to foster a pastor-dominated, sermon-driven worship machine that actually hinders the average player's role in Kingdom expansion? It's like the age-old tension of experience and opportunity. Remember when you couldn't get a job because of a lack of experience? And yet you couldn't get experience because no one would give you a job?

If the question is asked, "How will they hear without a preacher?" should another question also be asked, "How will they ever get good at preaching if the professional pastors do all the preaching for themselves?"

I have simply concluded that too many years of doing it the same way, too much tuition monies spent on seminary training, and too many books cracked on the subject of preaching make us feel as though we have to continue to reinforce the pastor's preeminent performance in the pulpit. After all, isn't that what the pastors were trained to do? Isn't that what pastors are paid for? It is very possible that too much tradition and the reinforcement of that tradition force us to continue to overstate the role as preacher and teacher. So we continue to be mesmerized by contests for the best preachers and the biggest audiences, rather than looking for more effective ways to release the church as a whole to do their best in growing and penetrating their culture.

Professor Robert Webber sees it like this, "I began to see that much of our worship is dominated by the pastor. From early childhood, I have been accustomed to the pastor doing everything. But in the past few years, I've noticed that I have become particularly sensitive to pastor-dominated worship services. Whenever I worship or speak at a church where the pastor is the focal point, I feel dominated and stifled. I find myself longing to participate, to be involved. I want to respond to what's going on, to say "Amen" or "Thanks be to God" or give witness to my faith or pray. But in churches where the pastor-figure is central, any response is often looked at as odd or inappropriate. In this situation my stomach actually feels tied up in knots, my muscles tense, and my whole body feels trapped, even caged in. My spirit and thus my worship are affected. I feel as though I'm not worshipping; I'm not actively participating. Rather, the pastor is doing everything for me. I'm simply a receiver, a passive recipient of the actions of another person."[1]

WORSHIP IS A VERB

According to Webber, in *Worship Is a Verb*, congregations dominated by the pastor or the pastoral staff become passive spectators; they begin to treat church meetings as just another form of entertainment, such as sitting down to watch television, attending a play, concert, or catching a dinner show. The reality is: Worship is a verb.

One day, strolling down the street next to our offices in San Diego, I was in conversation with a brother who was currently attending one of our house churches. We had just eaten breakfast together, and had enjoyed a really stimulating conversation over our meal. As we walked to our cars, I asked him about what the rest of his day looked like. He stated that he would be attending his house church that night, and commented that it was hard for him to attend. When I asked him "Why?" he said, "I think I like 'movie church,' you know, where you can just go and sit and watch and then leave, but in my house church they won't let me do that; they make you talk, they make you interact."

Teaching and training people to come to a gathering, knowing they are integral, necessary, and vital, is a far stretch from this movie-entertainment-type church. We have to instruct them (and believe me, it takes a lot of instruction and modeling) that they are there not just to observe, or to show mental assent, or to pay for services rendered as the plate is passed, but that they too are responsible for the quality and flow of the gathering. It takes a lot of time to convince them to fully engage and fully participate in this wonderful experience called "church."

This is an enormously difficult and timely pedagogy process. It doesn't just happen automatically, or even easily. The more you intentionally make room for others, the more you raise a new standard of possibilities for how meetings can go. But be warned, where some may feel uncomfortable, even threatened, many will like it, even many Westerners, and especially many of the MTV generation. As people are drawn upon to now see themselves as a room full of resources that God has placed there for a more multifaceted meal, many will shift in their mind-set and actually come to the meetings carrying their gifts. They will want, and even expect to be given the opportunity of sharing their gifts with the Body.

DIFFERENT DELIVERY SYSTEMS

So again, in one sense, it is not about getting the Word, the Bible, into a meeting. It is about how we do it. The shift away from the paid professional being the only delivery system is the issue. How about two sermons from two different individuals? Or even three? How about weaving together an exhortation, a teaching, a prophecy, and a testimony?

Two recent conversations with a couple leaders I am currently working with let me know that they were starting to get it. One came to me at the end of one of our meetings, as I had been challenging the people to participate more, and said, "Hey, Gary, how about telling us or letting us know the actual text you or whoever will be speaking on next week, so we can pray over and study the text at home, and see if God gives us anything to share or add next week to the message?" Another brother pointed out to me that his sense was that the more prepared I came to the meeting, the less others felt adequate, particularly in the area of the teaching of the Word.

In a recent gathering, I was doing the talking. (I still am the "talking head" on occasions when I have a strong word and feel that God would have me to share it!) Before I began, I handed out two small laminated signs, each one carrying a single word, which was the theme of my sermon, talk, lecture, and homily for that day. I handed one to each side of the room where people were sitting. I told the people to simply look at these little signs and then pass them along to someone else. A few minutes later, I stopped and asked where the signs were and asked that person who had the sign to stand and give their definition of the word or theme on the sign. At first, there was some hesitation as everyone now realized the price that would be paid to have the sign in one's possession when I paused to ask for a definition. But after they got over the initial shock that I was actually soliciting feedback, this little exercise began to flow, and for many, even became fun. By the end of the talk, it was working so well that some people were holding on to the sign, or even wanted it back, because they so eagerly wanted to participate and add to the meeting.

Many nations of the world do not have the luxury of highly trained seminarians leading their meetings, and yet their churches are growing by leaps and bounds with the priesthood of the believers at full tilt. Here we are in a country that even has contests to determine the greatest preachers of its day, yet we have people coming to our meetings week after week without engaging, without participating, and thus without growing.

LEARNING THAT WORKS

For years I have taken pride in being a "lifelong learner." I am always reading the latest book (my wife tells me I read too much!), and I attend conferences, seminars, workshops, always wanting to learn more. Well then, what about the people I am leading? I not only know they want to learn more, I also know that they will learn best when they are allowed to put into action or practice what they are learning. That includes sharing, even in a public church gathering, what God is showing them, or what they are getting from Him, and how it is working in their lives.

Do we heed today's prophets, today's prognosticators when they warn us that times have changed, and that we must change with the times? I wonder, what kind of systems are we creating when we, the preachers, eating hearty, healthy biblical meals during our weekly studies, live only to regurgitate these meals into smaller rations for the masses of openmouthed baby birds during the all-important Sunday morning feeding frenzy? Or, have we really been called to create learning colonies, or learning societies where people receive and release, and where they get it and give it away? The final test, or the final contest as to whether we are good at what we are doing is found in the end product of that shy, untrained, neophyte standing up in a worship celebration and sharing some thoughts that have deeply affected his life and proportionately now impact those in attendance—not because we as leaders are lazy, or bored, or burnt-out, but because we have intentionally planned the meetings so that others are encouraged to fully participate.

For years, I felt that my worth, at least in this current church system, was based upon my ability to succeed in my weekly, perfunctory performance as the professionally-trained preaching machine. And perform I did, from the earliest days of long periods of research and preparation not only for each message in my new series, but also taking complete responsibility for each part I played (and others played) in that one-and-a-half hour meeting.

Even as a worship-leading lad in my father's church, I was diligent to make sure I had a cute story about each hymn I led, and at least a verse or comment for each chorus. I took this call to lead seriously. And I still do. It is just that I am trying to lead differently now.

HELPING PEOPLE "GET IT"

Over these last few years we have been experimenting with many different kinds of gatherings, for different kinds of purposes and outcomes. And I am forever learning, debriefing, and learning again. Before we attempted some of these new and creative modes of learning, we first had to admit that a lot of what we had been doing had not been working all that well, or at least not working as well as it could. So how much longer will we perpetuate the model of the glazed-over looks of non-connected listeners as they stare at the overly compensated communicators?

C'mon, we can do better than that!—particularly as we take seriously our mandate to prepare God's people for works of service, so that the Body of Christ may be built up until we all reach unity in the faith and in the knowledge of the Son of God and become mature, attaining to the whole measure of the fullness of Christ (see Eph. 4:11-13). Because the purpose of the Church is people development, not just pastor performance, we must return to a biblical model that discourages spectators and applauds participators, without negating any gift of grace God wants to use to build us up, including His use of the Ephesians 4:11 ministry gifts.

A NEW WAY OUT

As pastors, your job in this new way of doing church, if you choose to take it, is even greater and more far-reaching than before. As mentors, coaches, and facilitators, you get to create an atmosphere and coach a team, rather than isolate yourself behind your own research and preplanned sermons. You get to break the predictability of that three-point homily and lead an equipped and empowered army to war.

Will you ever preach again? Of course you will and maybe even better. Sometimes you'll wrap up or apply what the Father has been saying, through many in any given meeting. Sometimes you'll have such a burning word that you will have to give it. But, it will come out of your heart of combustion in the prophetic moment, not the canned, preplanned sermon you recently downloaded from the Internet.

I quit listening to the bare contents of sermons a long time ago. What I do now, is listen for what it is that that person "carries." What is their life message? What is burning in them so hot it cannot be quenched? As God raises up spiritual fathers and mothers these days, this next generation needs to get what we "carry."

Rather than a neurotic need to control a meeting, we get to carry a fatherly release and give permission to others in our gatherings. Rather than the meeting being always about us, it is about them, and thus, ultimately about Him. How does the Father want to speak to us today? What is His agenda? What does He want to say? And whom does He want to say it through? Now, that's church!

ENDNOTE

1. Robert Webber, *Worship Is a Verb* (Peabody, MA: Hendrickson Publishers, 1992), 3.

Chapter Thirteen

A New Wineskin of Learning

DESPITE what some people think, as we move along in this continuum called the Third-Day Church, it really becomes very practical and not nearly as mystical or weird as it may appear. We are basically experimenting in our gatherings with the growing issue of extended worship expressions and the mutually edifying participation by the released "saints movement."

The worship is unrushed, unencumbered, extended, open, passionate, and highly experiential. This worship is for our Father, and it is to be worship that pleases Him, and worship that He leads. Next to that, there is an open invitation for others to participate and carry their gifts to the meeting for the purpose of mutual edification, requiring the creation of a new environment, new rules, and new patterns as we do church.

As we keep taking a long hard look at how we have done church for years, we must be willing to grapple with all forms of "scaly skin" that need to become a new wineskin. As I mentioned in the last chapter, the last bastion of resistance usually falls into this area of preaching or teaching, or at least how and when we preach or teach. It is here where we bump into some of our strongest habits, with adjustments and changes needed. To be willing to touch that all-but-sacred, single-pastor, lecture-driven form, we begin by asking some hard questions about our philosophy of how people learn.

So let's ask some of those hard questions. Are there more effective ways of communicating besides one-sided lectures? What did God have in mind for the local church pastor-preacher-orator? Is he or she to be the resident theologian, pumping out homilies like a Pez dispenser? Or was His goal much more of the coach-player, facilitator-mentor model? And if the latter is true, how do we shift from all of those years of serious study patterns, and open up to a brand-new world of interactive, dialogue-driven messages?

SHIFTS HAPPEN

If we are committed to consciously and intentionally reaching the people in our meetings, calling them to participate, and creating an environment for them to play in, we have to make some changes. I do know that the success or failure of some highly interactive meetings often does depend on the numeric size of the gathering. But the bigger issue seems to be around the preparedness of the people's hearts for a new "talking church" shift in the meetings. And that means a radical shift in the leader's own heart and passion to change, in order to help facilitate the part or parts that others can play in these meetings.

All this is based, of course, upon the assumption or conviction that you believe the priesthood of the believers should be experienced in today's church. Again, I have personally witnessed the direct correlation between a believer's participation level in meetings and/or gatherings, and that individual's boldness, aggressiveness, and sense of identity and calling as they live out their Christian walk or life on a day-by-day basis.

I feel it is time to declare a moratorium on the droning, lecture-only lifestyle of our present meetings, in which the Hebraic-style open meetings of the first-century Church has given way to Greek and Roman intellectual reasoning through lecture and one-way oratory by the clergy class.

And we need to take a fresh, hard look at creating new meetings that will move towards the collegiate model of First Corinthians

14:26, where everyone is a potential contributor to the meeting. And where that does not necessarily mean that everyone will contribute, it does mean that they all have the potential or possibility or opportunity to contribute.

BECOMING SOCRATIC

Beginning to shift away from the predictable lecture-listen style of communication to more of an experimental and experiential form may simply include looking and adjusting ever so slightly our current delivery systems.

People in this postmodern era seem to have a stigma about being "preached at." Biblical communication with some of that "preachy" edge removed gets us repositioned (at least in the perception of postmodern people), as we shift passive-pew sitters into mutual ministers.

Moving away from the pure monologue style of teaching or preaching is a no-brainer when you consider that your audience has drastically changed. In fact, just trying to "know your audience" is a start. To ignore this "listener shift" in today's culture is suicide. Too often this addiction or "subject stubbornness" is epitomized by our preaching along lines week after week that are not even germane to the needs of the very people we are trying to teach.

It is critical then, that our meetings, and our presentation, and our style of communicating fit the needs of our current audience.

Capturing the principles of a multi-sensory mosaic culture where people get fed through different streams—audibly (what you hear), visually (what you see), and kinesthetically (what you feel and touch)—is critical. Leonard Sweet has offered us a modern acrostic that sets the stage for a whole new approach to learning.

He calls it *EPIC*: "experience," "participation," "image," and "connected." Become a storyteller, connecting with people's emotions and not just their brains. Tell your information, but also your experience, not just your perceptions and propositions, but also your feelings.

Telling it with humor, even sarcasm, helps them catch it, and when you tell it like a journey, it makes more sense of their own pilgrimage.[1]

Make sure that your messages are not just doctrinally pure and exegetically accurate, but also make sure your messages are challenging intellectually, spiritually, emotionally, even socially. Yes, do all those neat creative things that we are so good at these days with video, audio, drama, etc., but also make sure that you yourself are passionate and dynamic, as they catch you, the messenger and not just the message. This audience is not just looking to be entertained; they are looking to be engaged.

Another way to help you have a paradigm shift in your own thinking about a more effective teaching model is to remember the old principles of what has been called "quadruple think."

In *quadruple think*, you:

1) Think out what you have to say.

2) Then think how the other person(s) will understand what you have to say.

3) Then rethink what you have to say.

4) So that when you say it, they will end up thinking what you are thinking.

As we develop a workable Q & A style, using the classic Socratic approach of asking questions that solicit more than just a "yes" or "no" answer, we actually step into an ancient form of communication that continues to yield great benefit in this biblical process of inquiry.

OPEN MEETINGS ARE NOT NEW

Deuteronomy 17:9 states: *"Go to the priests, who are Levites, and to the judge who is in office at that time. Inquire of them and they will give you the verdict"* (NIV). "Inquire" is the Hebrew word *darash*, which means "to question or to search." Such inquiry was later developed in the synagogue as a "Beit Midrash" or house of study. "Midrash" conveys this idea of investigation and research and discussion.

Jesus taught by asking open-ended questions like, "Who do men say that I am?" "Whose likeness is on your coin?" "Which one was this man's neighbor?" Stop in the middle of your message and become a roving reporter by taking the microphone to the people and interview them by asking what they are hearing.

Seek out current testimonies, asking for the "been there, done that" of life. It adds great credibility and strength to the point you are trying to get across. I am told that Rick Warren of Saddleback Community Church in Mission Viejo, California, uses testimonies every week to increase the impact of his messages. Know what is going on in your audience; ask for praise reports. Request e-mails on a regular basis that come to you informing you of the Kingdom victories that are all around you.

A basic return to a "Socratic Community," where we learn to ask questions rather than always dispensing answers is a quantum leap in becoming better at communicating truth, and to stop preaching in the dark.

I know firsthand that this takes work, and believe me, it won't happen overnight. It requires much creative debriefing all along the way. But it's worth it! Even the simplest shift of asking questions changes the whole atmosphere of a meeting. It says loud and clear that everyone is valuable to this process of body life—that all of us have a contribution to make.

Start living in a dialogue mentality, looking at people's faces and their nonverbal responses. And don't be afraid if it appears that they are not getting it. Don't be afraid to stop; don't be afraid to be vulnerable and ask them if you are making sense. And even be willing to ask them if your message is really as boring as it sounds to you.

SURPRISE: YOU'RE THE GUEST SPEAKER!

One meeting, I began to speak by introducing my subject and then announced that we had five different guest speakers in today's meeting, although they did not know who they were yet. I then commenced to present the key point, the summary of the subject, the sound bite, and then wandered around the room from one handpicked person to another handpicked person with my microphone and requested their "take" on what I had just said.

It was quite surprising. After the initial awkwardness and the clearing of throats, people really got into it. And I assure you, for weeks to come, people listened better, maybe out of the fear that any week I would do this again.

My father told me of his early preaching classes at Bible college. He said that the students were advised to stare at a spot on the back wall of the building and to not look at the people's faces. This, of course, was a method of preacher-protection knowing that people's faces could convey confusion, anger, or obvious disagreement. And if they did, you might change your emphasis, your point, or your whole sermon.

I have called this "Lamaze preaching," like getting a birthing mother fixated on a spot on the wall to take her attention off some of the pains of her contractions. But instead of doing that, why not use their responses to teach you whether or not they are getting it and how you could enhance your skill as a communicator? If that is too risky, at least ask them for feedback, either at the end of the message or maybe at the beginning of the next time you share with them.

Of course, some of you are far ahead of the game in creative learning, using drama vignettes, role-plays, narratives, monologues, humor, video clips, asking for questions and answers, debate, and overall feedback. And you can get as creative as you want, as long at it works. People experience more, learn more, retain more, and are transformed more when they are encouraged to participate in the reciprocal process of giving and receiving in these third-day meetings. And we, too, as leaders, are challenged to grow more when we accept the honest feedback of the people we are trying to reach.

MENTORING THAT MATTERS

I would like to suggest that we even change our whole approach to equipping others. Let's do it by intentional mentoring. Rather than spending our entire time running the church as it is with the demand for fresh bread or new life-changing weekly sermons, let's mentor, coach, and equip the next generation of great preachers. Every leader I know who has been leading any length of time has developed what are called "life messages." These are subjects that are your passion; these are the things others know you for; this is what you leak and drip on others.

Well, get intentional and build entire communication systems around these truths that you carry. Get that group of people who are always following you around, always asking questions, always wanting to pick your brain, always wanting more, and put them in your life intentionally and consistently.

Mentoring is a relational experience in which one person empowers another by sharing God-given resources.

Mentoring is a process of helping a person grow according to a plan which reflects the person's needs over a flexible, but definite period of time, and focuses on a goal of becoming a laborer in that person's context of life and ministry.

WEARING YOUR NEW HAT

We know mentoring is why Jesus chose the twelve; we know that people learn best in these smaller contextual environments. So change hats, simply from the larger-crowd lecturer/feeder, to the smaller-team coach/trainer. You will be surprised what happens to you when you simply put on a baseball cap and start hanging out with those who want to play ball.

I have learned these days to design most of my time around other leaders in the context of their lives, spending individual time over coffee, but also in small mentoring groups, walking them through some of my life messages. I am especially concerned with developing their personal history with God through teaching and modeling to them contemplative reading, personal worship, and journaling. Too many burnt-out friends who I care for operate solely out of a corporate identity, or who they are when they are in front of a group of people, rather than the sense they have of who they are before God, being His friend, spending enormous amounts of time with Him.

We give reading assignments to these leaders and then get together and discuss what we have read. We even do the discussion in public coffeehouses. We call this "extreme caffeine"! Sure, all of this takes time, but I am actually finding it more rewarding that my normal Sunday blasts. It is like the difference between a shotgun blast, hoping some of it will hit, and a precision target where I can see and experience the penetration marks.

So put your baseball cap on—it is time to change hats. One of my favorite old-time TV comedians was Jonathan Winters. As part of his act, he would go into a room with a bunch of different hats hanging everywhere. As he put on each hat, he would spontaneously act out the new character that fit the unique hat. Like Winters, we can learn to change hats and roles as quickly as society demands. The shifts in today's culture are many; changes are happening fast, from the rational to the experiential, and from observation to revelation. What it means is that we stay flexible and creative, listening, watching, and responding to what is in front of us, not just behind us.

ENDNOTE

1. Leonard Sweet, *EPIC*, http://www.next-wave.org/may00/ sweet.htm.

Section Six

THIRD-DAY MISSION

Chapter Fourteen

AN UNTAINTED MISSION

FOR almost four decades, it has been my privilege and my personal adventure to participate in international travel. In the early days, the degree of concern and the risk of any given short-term missions trip was summarized in "don't drink the water," "buy an abundant supply of bug repellant," and "wear a good hat to keep you protected from the sun." The risks are now far more serious and sophisticated, having escalated to political persecution and terrorism, as Western missionaries have been taken hostage, brutalized, and even murdered.

But, I wonder if one of the greatest risks to traveling outside the contiguous 48 states is, in reality, the fact that you have to come face-to-face with this Western addiction to religious forms and traditions, and the ways we so deftly superimpose these forms on the rest of the world. Like a new breed of apologists, when you arrive on foreign soil you end up first having to do some kind of damage control, often finding that that unique culture has been violated by the church itself. In the wake of our imposition of a foreign model into this raw tribal venue, I wonder if we should call it "messiology" instead of "missiology."

PARADISE LOST?

And this happens in more than just your classic Third World setting. How about our own beautiful 50th state, the islands of Hawaii? According to the article, "Hawaii" in the December 2002 issue of

National Geographic, as early as the 1820s, not long after the first missionaries arrived from New England, cultural suppression immediately began with the banning of the hula, because its dancing and chanting was connected to the Hawaiian gods—Kane, the creator; Lono, god of harvests; and Ku, the god of war.

Totally dismissing the fact that the hula was at the heart of Hawaiian culture, and was actually the art of retelling the story of history and creation, missionaries deemed the expression offensive. In fact, the whole Hawaiian language itself would be extinct today were it not for some who refused to lose their voice in the two centuries since the missionaries came ashore. In the past two decades, many more have begun to pay attention to a culture where the highest compliment you can pay someone is to write a song about him or her or sing a song to them. Hmm…sounds like worship to me![1]

My ongoing itinerary and sorties to other places and other lands continue to push my "modern-missions tolerance envelope" over the edge. I have been forced to reexamine my heart and my motives for taking the message I have and what I carry to other lands, cultures, tribes, and tongues. I am committed to looking deeply into all our current Western forms and questioning their supposed sacredness. This is not done in a mean-spirited way, as much as in an honest attempt to be free from the cultural bondages of the past so that we might be able see how we can more effectively reach this new millennium harvest. To say that I am grieved over what I have found on my travels is to put it mildly. Lately, I have been flat out horrified.

An unusual question must be asked: Are you able to communicate with different people groups in a way that they can understand you? Or is your paradigm so strong that you know only one language? Let me ask it another way: Is the rubric for your Christianity (the paradigm, the focus) so American, so Western, that your package and your presentation simply cannot change?

THE QUEST TO BRING SOMETHING PURE

Sure, it is hard to perceive of ministering to a different culture without affecting or influencing them. But to take an honest message of biblical Christianity to other shores means that we must enter the battle of substance versus style, and essence versus expression in order to leave them something pure, untainted, and uncontaminated.

I know we bring them something on these important missionary trips. But does it have to be a worn-out religious practice, another lifeless church form, even a tried-but-not-true expression? Or do we want to give them the purest essence, the truest heart, the most honest biblical value, and then trust the Holy Spirit to express that value through them in such a way that is culturally relevant for them, not us?

Roland Allen, in his classic, *Missionary Methods, St. Paul's or Ours?* addresses this whole battle of form versus essence, style versus substance, and external versus internal, as well as anyone. He notes that as missionaries, we have tended to offer the externals first, the props, the trappings. Because of this habit, it becomes too easy for new converts to then put the external in the place of the internal. For example, attendance at a certain kind of house of prayer might even take the place of prayer itself.

Allen adds that it is easy to mistake the provision of the ornaments of worship for the duty of worship. We bring these ornaments, or fixtures, or practices of our worship forms because they often have meaning behind them, at least to us. But the heathen naturally looks at religion from a different point of view. When he sees the externals provided at a cost that seems to him very great, and things imported, which his own country cannot provide, he inevitably tends to suppose that our religion is as his own.[2]

BOTCHED ORGAN TRANSPLANT

To me, it is like the proverbial "gift with strings attached." Have you ever received one of those gifts that you just knew would, in the end, come back to "bite" you? For example, during my first trip to Central America in the early 1970s, I noticed an organ in this little mountain church in this extremely impoverished country. It wasn't just any organ, but an old-fashioned pump organ. The problem was, no one really knew how to play it. But because it was a gift, they kept it, and in fact, it was a centerpiece in this little rustic chapel. These mountain Christians, with men sitting on one side and women on the other (Gee, I wonder where they got that idea?) normally sang accapella, and beautiful, four-part-harmony accapella at that. So, they discovered a rare use for the organ. They simply picked out their harmony parts by playing that particular key on the organ.

At each service, someone would first pump the pump organ until there was enough air in the bellows and then touch each of the harmony keys, and finally that individual would run around the organ to join the singers. I guess you had to do something with that organ. After all, someone gave it as a gift, and it was an expensive gift. So that is how a Central American tribal people who sang accapella, used a foreign-made, cumbersome, bulky, church pump organ.

We travel thousands of miles and spend thousands of dollars to reach far-off lands where these cultures have existed for years, long before us, and we bring them the Gospel, the Good News—the Good News that we are saved by grace through faith, that they too can trust in the finished work of the Cross, that Christ paid the price in full, and that it is "the Cross plus nothing." Then we make these new Christians dependent on us as we make sure they have our church buildings, our church furniture, our Western instruments (like pump organs), our platforms, with our platform chairs and pulpits, and our PA systems. Then, of course, they have to have special clothing, they have to sing our hymns, they have to use our children's curriculum, etc., ad nausea. Oh, they are saved by grace through faith alone, and now we give them all of these trappings to make them real Christians, or at least Christians just like us.

Have we missed the point that they have their own music, their own dance, and their own songs, and are gifted, often rhythmic people with their own native instruments? Have we forgotten the fact that they move and sway as a cultural expression, sing accapella, and/or maybe don't even sing at all, but chant or clap or click or whistle or sign?

This is one of the chiefest and most insidious of our difficulties in modern missions. Allen goes on to add, "By importing and using and supplying to the natives buildings and ornaments and that which they cannot procure for themselves, we tend to pauperize the converts. They cannot supply what they think to be needful, and so they learn to accept the position of passive recipients."

I thought we took care of this issue in that famous Jerusalem Council in Acts 15. Wasn't that stuff all settled back then? This whole idea of making Gentiles into Jews in order to make them Christians— wasn't that settled then, in that first Council, with Peter's confession about Cornelius' house, and the response of the Holy Spirit through James? Or was it? Isn't there room for uniqueness, for differences? Now, is that a bad thing? Or does everything and everybody have to be alike? For all of this current medical/ethical debate around cloning, I wonder if that is what we are still doing? Aren't we really saying, most of the time, that in order for you to be a "real" Christian, you must act, dress, and worship just like me?

FORMLESSNESS IS DANGEROUS

I do believe God gave us forms. He gave us patterns, and He gave us practices. In fact, to preach a "formless faith" is to be like some kind of esoteric oxymoron. The whole issue of being without "form" is extremely dangerous, for when creation was "without form," it was also "void" (see Gen. 1:2). Interestingly, though, the same God, who gave us sacrificial patterns and practices, also grew weary of their lifeless abuse. *"I have had enough of burnt offerings of rams and the fat of fed cattle. I do not delight in the blood of bulls, or of lambs or goats"* (Isa. 1:11b). I am not saying that we should do away with all forms, or even all traditions. It is just that our forms and traditions must support our values, and have life to them, and not become dead ritual.

One of the signs of an apostate church in the last days is that people will *"have a form of godliness, but deny its power"* (2 Tim. 3:5a). Jesus even warned the religious people of His day that they had actually neutered the Word by their repetitive, habitual religious traditions, making it "of no effect" (see Matt. 15:6).

ASKING THE HARDER QUESTIONS

I was recently informed by a brother of his concern about whether or not we embraced important practices or traditions, or what he called "marks of the church," which were instituted by Jesus and His apostles. He made reference to the Lord's Supper, baptism, prayer, the exposition of Scripture, readings of Scripture, church discipline, and the preaching of the Gospel.

I assured him that we do all of these things. And in addition, we are asking the harder questions of how and when and where do we do them? And we don't want to fall into the trap of a one-size-fits-all syndrome, concerning what we choose to do, lest our vision become bigger than God's.

ENDNOTES

1. Theroux, Paul. "Hawaii", *National Geographic Magazine*, December 2002.

2. Roland Allen, *Missionary Methods, St. Paul's or Ours?* (Grand Rapids, MI: Eerdmans, 1962), 52-54.

Chapter Fifteen

QUESTIONS OF VALUE

I am not exactly sure when or where you were drafted into the "worship wars" of today's church. Personally, I wasn't enlisted at all; I was born into the fray. Being raised in the classical camp of old-time Pentecostalism, my elders had a cow (and it wasn't sacred!) when mainline denominations entered the Charismatic Renewal in the 1960s, and began receiving the fullness of the Spirit, tongues and all. Then came the neo-charismatics, and what a shock when I, myself, left my heritage to join the "third wave."

The debate indicates we have now entered the age of the neo-apostolic. One might have thought we would have learned some big lessons along the way, like the one that God is a whole lot bigger than our personal doctrinal box, but I don't think so!

THE LEFT-BRAIN GAME

The "proof-texting" debacle around the manifestations of the Toronto Blessing in the mid-1990s, for example, led us right back into another exercise in futility. It seems that everything in our left-brain culture, which is addicted to logic, analysis, and the need for empirical explanation, jumped ahead of us once again. Having become inundated in America culture, with its anti-supernatural worldview, we ignorantly plodded along like robots trying to scientifically explain everything.

In the face of all the different, and sometimes bizarre manifestations, we once again began this "chapter and verse crossword puzzle." After all, we had to have concrete, black-and-white biblical reasons for every "renewal manifestation," whether it be laughing, falling backward or forward, crying, shaking, jerking, appearing drunken, etc.

These "manifestations," or "affections," as they were called during the Great Awakenings, are not to be made doctrine, or science; however, we once again put on our linguistic research hats, and dove into that abyss of analysis. We were determined to find and highlight any obscure verse that might shed some light on these extreme expressions in order to defend or attack them. And once again we pulled the parking brake on the present move of God as we entered into the matrix of our own making, stuck in that Christian cul-de-sac of anti-supernatural intellectualism. And to what end? Because as soon as we got one manifestation nailed down, another one, far more bizarre, jumped out of the box!

Meantime, we missed the whole basic hermeneutical principle of "primary text" (what is consistent in Scripture), and the principle of "secondary text" (what is inconsistent in Scripture).[1] When it comes to the different and varied responses to God's manifest presence, yes, we do have a God who is alive, who is revelatory, and who shows up and touches us. And when He does, when you sense His presence or feel His touch, it may cause a reaction, an expression, or a physical manifestation. But the fact that the very manifestation which you are experiencing may appear very different than the manifestation of the person next to you who is at the same time experiencing the same God and the same Holy Spirit, is a reminder that when God visits, what happens next is up to Him and you.

I have often thought that, rather than trying to defend or judge "pet" manifestations over the years, it is easier to respond to the question, "Hey, look, is that God?" by answering, "Well, that is how that person is responding to and/or experiencing God's manifest presence."

PRIMARY PRINCIPLES

Let's go back to this principle of "primary text." Let's take something as universally recognized and important as baptism. Jesus preached it, He commanded it, and He even subjected Himself to it. Now what about the when, where, and how of baptism? We must be careful to not turn too quickly our personal preference into a science, a doctrine, or a point of division. We have to allow baptism to remain contextual to the culture, the season, the moment, and the personal tradition. If we let our personal form take precedence over the "primary text," we end up preaching, fighting, and defending our own strict formula. I think we've had enough scrimmages over this one.

Yes, let's baptize! And even if you are personally convinced of the point that the mere mention that *"Jesus, immediately coming up from the water"* (see Mark 1:10) puts in concrete for you that this is the only way to be baptized, the questions still remain: What time of day? River, ocean, creek, hot tub, swimming pool, or baptismal fount? Do you go in face-forward or backward? Who does the baptizing? Is it the priest, the pastor, the parent? Do you wear special clothing or just street clothes? And of course, these are lightweight issues compared to the ongoing battle that continues to be waged over the Matthew 28:19 and Acts 2:3 formulas.

My point, believe it or not, is actually simpler than you think. I remember the words of the musician who was once asked what was greater—knowledge or wisdom. "Without knowledge," he answered, "I could not play the violin. Without wisdom, I could not play the music." So for me, the knowledge of a certain form, be it baptism, communion, prophecy, or musical instruments in worship, is only part of the equation, as wisdom takes its turn to discern when, where, and how these forms are to be expressed.

I guess I have assumed that you, like me, have been asking these harder questions for years. So in case you haven't, please humor me as I get a little redundant here, and give you some of the questions we could be asking.

Please don't pass out or start hyperventilating. This is not a sacrilegious act. This is simply letting God adjust our preconceived ideas about what we do. Jesus' encounter with the woman at the well is an example. He set some things clear as He informed her that the place of worship, the tradition, the history, and the forms have changed— that it is not about worshiping in this mountain, or a Samaritan one, or a Jewish one; but it is about the essence, the heart, the spirit of worship (see John 4:23-24).

We have to ask these harder questions, so that at the end of the day, our values dictate our form or forms, rather than the opposite. We must constantly fight to lessen the gap between our orthodoxy (what we believe) and our orthopraxy (what we do). We must make sure we remain open to God's leading, and to the cultural context, when we engage in these things that we value. And we must ask these hard questions if we want to more effectively reach the current harvest.

So for those of us who are tired of being stuck in one way of "doing church," and are frankly tired of the "McChurch" franchising of modern church planting, let's look at what we do in our times of gathering, and more importantly, let's get in touch with our true "values" to make sure what we are doing is in keeping with those values, whether that be corporate worship, the Word, communion, gathering, prophecy, healing, giving, or evangelism.

ABOUT THE VALUE OF CORPORATE WORSHIP

- Do we worship with an orchestra, a choir, a praise team, or a song leader?
- Do we worship with a mixture of instruments, just an organ or piano, or accapella?
- Are the musical instruments to be amplified or acoustic?

- Are the musical instruments we use to be Western in style, or can they be cross-cultural, even tribal?

- Does the worship team stand in front, at the back, or in the middle of the building?

- Is the worship rehearsed or spontaneous?

- Is the worship leading for just the worship leaders or others in the congregation?

- Do we use prerecorded music, CDs or cassettes, or only live music?

- Do we sing hymns, choruses, or both?

- Do we project the words through overhead projectors, Powerpoint presentations, or print the lyrics?

- Is there to be a set liturgy, or a free flow?

- How long is the worship, and what are the time limits?

- When does the worship occur—before or after the preaching?

ABOUT THE VALUE OF THE TAUGHT WORD

- Do we teach every week, or once a month, or on an as-needed basis?

- Are the teachers pastors, seminary trained educators, or anyone God speaks through?

- Do we teach in the main meeting, seminars, classes, conferences?

- Do we teach by lecture, discussion, illustration, debate, directed interaction, Q & A?

- Do we teach verse-by-verse, expositional, topical, textual?

- Do we teach in small groups or large groups or every time we meet?
- Do we teach to inform, to equip, to empower?
- Do we teach before or after the worship?
- How long should the sermon be—20 minutes, 30 minutes, 45 minutes, 60-plus minutes?

ABOUT THE VALUE OF COMMUNION

- Is it to be celebrated in special meetings or all meetings?
- Is it a small group experience, large group experience, or both?
- Do we practice communion in our homes or just in the sanctuary?
- Is it to be treated as a full agape meal or as a religious snack?
- Do we use wine, grape juice, or both?
- What about the bread...rolls, crackers, matzo?
- Do we use a single cup or many small cups?
- If we use a single cup, should we dip the bread in the cup, or sip the cup?
- Who administers this tradition—the pastor, priest, or the priesthood of all?
- Do we do it before, during, or after the other parts of the service?
- Do we do it on the first Sunday of the month or every week?

ABOUT THE VALUE OF GATHERING

- Do we gather in homes, warehouses, schools, hotels, parks, bars, pubs, restaurant, or church buildings?
- Do we gather on Saturday, Sunday, or any other day of the week?
- Do we gather every weekend or on an as-needed basis?
- Do the professional clergy lead these meetings, or are they open for participation from the body?
- Do we have worship, teaching, and personal ministry, and in what order?
- When there is teaching, who does it—the clergy or the saints?
- What do we do with children during these gathered times?
- Who teaches and disciples the children?
- Do the gatherings last one hour, two hours, three hours, all day?

ABOUT THE VALUE OF PROPHECY

- Do we prophesy from the front of the building?
- Do we use the microphone to prophesy?
- Do we prophesy in small groups?
- When someone prophesies, who discerns or judges the prophecy?
- Who gets to prophesy? Is it the tested prophet, the neophyte, any believer?

- Is it public, private, personal, directional, corrective, directive?
- Is it national, regional, local?

ABOUT THE VALUE OF HEALING

- Do we use a healing evangelist?
- Do we use a prayer or ministry team?
- Do we use elders, and how do we define "elder"?
- Do we do it with the Lord's Supper or Eucharist?
- Do we use words of knowledge?
- Do we use anointing oil? How much oil?
- Do we use special water?
- Do we use aprons or prayer cloths?
- Do we use fasting and prayer?
- Do we use confession of sin?
- Do we use spiritual warfare?

ABOUT THE VALUE OF GIVING

- Do we teach the tithe?
- Do we teach from the Old Testament, or the New Testament, or both?
- Do we teach the storehouse tithe or the worship tithe?
- Do we teach tithes and offerings?

- Do we give to the poor?
- Do we give to the widows?
- Do we give to world missions?
- Do we give to leaders?
- Of the fivefold ministries, who do we give the most to? Or do they all receive based upon their needs?

ABOUT THE VALUE OF EVANGELISM

- Do we do mass evangelism?
- Do we do personal evangelism?
- Do we do presence evangelism?
- Do we do power evangelism?
- Do we do servant evangelism?
- Do we do neighborhood evangelism?
- Do we do "oikos" evangelism?
- Do we distribute evangelistic literature?
- Do we hire staff evangelists?

A MATTER OF CHOICE

As you look at these lists (and believe me, I do not consider them exhaustive), I am sure you can find your favorite forms, your least favorite ones, and even your most hated. But that is just the point. Certain chosen forms, as important and special, and even as needed as we might think they are, are often chosen because of taste, or style, or setting, or cultural preference, or denominational tradition. Now, in one sense, it is not all bad to have your favorite forms, your favorite order of service, or your "auto pilot mode" of doing church.

Go ahead and choose your favorite forms. The challenge is to go beyond them. Remember the famous last eight words of the church— "We have never done it that way before!" So go beyond your comfort zone and your own favorites enough to address any form of passivity or form of rigidity. Go far enough to allow all your religious buttons to get fully hammered. Go ahead and choose your favorite forms. Just remember, those forms are not necessarily sacred. They are not necessarily divine. And even let the forms shift, change, vary, or even die. It's the values that we are after, keeping those values front and center.

So here is your mission—your third-day mission, if you choose it: Take the pure, simple, and yet potent message of the Gospel to your friends next door and to the nations of the world.

Give it away without the baggage or the trappings of your pet style, your organized method, or your stale religious form! When you travel to these far-off exotic places, these new cultures and these new lands, ask God to show you what He is already doing in that particular place, culture, and people group. And, please don't make them American Christians. Instead, enjoy how God has made each one of them, delighting in Him as He uses them in His way for His glory.

ENDNOTE

1. Bill Jackson, *What in the World Is Happening to Us?*, (Champaign Vineyard Chritian Fellowship, 1994), http://evanwiggs.com/revival/manifest/holylaff.html.

Chapter Sixteen

CHURCH: SIMPLE AND REGIONAL

L ANGUAGE is amazing! Terminology these days requires an ever-ready openness to nuances and shifts. To merely be able to spot, discern, and define what we hear requires almost a technological, digital retuning of our ears. You literally have to be some kind of a word-smith to basically attempt to function as a leader in today's market-place. The nomenclature and semantics change with the ever shifting tide of culture and communication. Even though we speak a dialect, a definitive language, the language seems to be forever changing. Remember when "bad" meant "good," and "gross" meant "great"?

Just think of the words that have evolved from our day to this one. Dictionaries have to be updated like newspapers. When you dare to speak with young people (actually, anyone younger than yourself), or rather, listen, you almost need a translator. And definitely don't try to really get into their music. To even try to listen to it confirms that people still speak in tongues in this dispensation.

In my current glossary of ecclesiastical lingo, I have become very fond of these two words: simple and regional. Both have become more than just catch phrases for me in this season, but also "word pictures" that address both form and function in how I do church.

Years ago, I made the discovery like so many of you, that in terms of an audience, when Paul, in his epistles, addressed the churches to whom he was writing, each particular church was inevitably defined or outlined or set as a church in a specific "region." Every letter he writes has this simple, yet unmistakable sequence. He always starts out with his apostolic resume, usually in verse one of that epistle and then, just like clockwork, he addresses the church in that region, whether Ephesus, or Galatia, Philippi, etc.

We learn from Paul that he understood that the New Testament concept of the church always referred to the church in that city or that region, and that his own personal revelation of his God-given influence had to do with the sphere of his apostolic assignment. He understood and accepted the obvious leadership and stewardship of his apostolic call just as much as he understood the clear limitations and boundaries of his own specific sphere. In First Corinthians 9:1-2a he questions, *"Am I not an apostle? Am I not free? Have I not seen Jesus Christ our Lord? Are you not my work in the Lord? If I am not an apostle to others, yet doubtless I am to you."*

In his book, *Apostles and Prophets*, C. Peter Wagner notes that apostolic spheres can manifest themselves as ecclesiastical spheres, like a certain number of churches or ministries; as functional spheres, with a leader having great influence in a certain area or type of ministry; and obviously geographical or territorial spheres, where someone has specific authority in a specific territory or region.[1]

GIFTING, CALLING, AND SPHERE

Having taught on the subject of "spiritual gifts" for so many years, I was often limited in both my explanation and intent to help others discover their gifting until I began to wrestle not only with the gift, but also with the calling, and even more lately the sphere.

So you have a calling to teach, which includes both your passion and your pursuit? What does the calling look like? First of all, whom do you teach? Young people, older people, tuition-driven students, graduate students, neophytes? And how do you teach? How does the gifting show up? Are you best as an instructor, a full-time professor, a bi-vocational mentor, or maybe as a researcher, a consultant, or even an author? And even when that is settled, what sphere is best for you to teach? Is it a small group, a large group, a church setting, a classroom setting, a boardroom setting, a committee setting, or a marketplace setting?

I have a deep desire to help people find their niche, their bent, and their groove. As a leader I found out, sometimes the hard way, that my gifting did better, was more effective, and quite frankly more enjoyable in certain settings, certain arenas, certain venues, certain spheres.

When I accepted the fact that I was not your typical local church parish pastor, I began to see my effectiveness increase proportionately. I began to see myself called to a region and longing to be a part of a regional church. I have been extremely encouraged, as I have learned that this modality, this model has taken effect around the world. It combines both of these new favorite words, not only as usable terminology but as clear definitions of how church works for me within my region.

REGIONAL CHURCH

Our response to the permissional message of doing church differently has included experimenting for years with groups of different sizes, different settings, different locations, and different formats. As mentioned in Chapter Eight, we felt more and more comfortable with these different ways of identifying our sphere and have learned that part of our call was to facilitate and bless, not to govern and control, the wonderful things God was doing in our region and in our case, our county.

This meant blessing what we saw the Father doing, encouraging people to step into their own passion and gifting, and then attempting to bring these groups of people together in such a way as one, not to compete with them; and two, to provide a base of unity and cohesiveness that would, in fact, enhance and help nurture and equip them in their own sphere (see Eph. 4).

To do this we began to experiment with a larger regional collective worship model, providing a place, an outlet for something that looked and felt very different than your average local church worship gathering. We shifted to an off-night, and moved this meeting to different parts of our region. And because we were not trying to be a local church, and definitely did not want to appear competitive with the many local churches in our community, we decided to meet once or twice per month, rather than weekly.

As we continue to gather in these larger regional settings, the dynamic is very different than your typical, weekend gathering of the local community church. We purposely cultivate a different feeling with an atmosphere of long and intensive prophetic worship. Because we are not trying to maintain a well-tuned weekend worship expression, we are very open to a variety of input that automatically makes it feel more like an event, a conference, and a rally.

Sometimes as the evening goes along, several people will take part in the preaching, or teaching, or sharing, rather than the typical one-man led meetings that we are so accustomed to. We do this because we realize that an atmosphere of extended prophetic worship is vital to receiving an impartation of the Holy Spirit that goes beyond a typical teaching session. There is no institution to join in these meetings; this is not a local church; it is regional church, church in the region. In fact, these meetings are not about the meetings, but about the bringing together of the wonderful variety of groups and ministries within our region. It is the coming together of these uniquely different expressions of the Body of Christ that make these meetings so different and so exciting.

This just might represent the best stewardship of the equipping gifts of Ephesians 4. In the regional team context, these leaders, or teams relate to an entire region, and the cross-pollinated Body of Christ within that whole region, rather than so many isolated community churches.

And for those actually traveling and doing itinerate equipping, it helps them to be able to focus on a whole region or cluster or network of churches rather than having to wear themselves out by the constant travel and marketing of themselves to a bunch of smaller meetings within churches in a given region that are not connected.

The historic church had two expressions of corporate life—small groups meeting in homes and some kind of gathering together of the Body of Christ within a given city or region. This paradigm of the "scattered church" in smaller meetings throughout the city and the "gathered church" where everyone comes together for something bigger, seems to fit the regular pattern of the New Testament Church.

There were no facility-based churches limited to their demographics as we see in local churches today. The isolation this brings is horrific. With congregations engaged in non-stop turf wars, the average group has no concept of being actually tied in Christ to the tribe or expression of God that meets in the competing building across the street.

And with the "bigger-is-better" mentality of American franchise marketing, everything comes down to the professionals, the platforms, the pulpits, the pews, the parking, and the public address systems. The question is: Who can pull off the best performance in town, and get the most people to come? And most pastors become the paid production managers to facilitate the stage crews who are hired to set up and tear down the weekend gig.

Christ gave some very specific people—apostles, prophets, evangelists, pastors and teachers—to do the one main and the one plain thing—equip the saints, with a body or church growing by the "every part," and "every joint" in this equipping system of Ephesians 4.

Whatever this means, "equipping the saints" is apparently their historic and current job description. With our present clergy-addicted system creating way too much spiritual unemployment, with hundreds, possibly even thousands, going to meetings every weekend only to become more "pew fodder," for the next "wanna-be" Mega-Church superstar it looks like the church itself is unemployed, and the equipping system of Ephesians 4 seems basically ignored.

Church: Simple and Regional addresses this bigger issue. The bigger issue is not form, or even size, or even where we meet, but the leadership of His Church, how the leaders lead, and the potential release of the priesthood of all believers within a region.

It means leaders creating an atmosphere for more people to lead, more people to grow, more people to be released—not just more believers in more meetings. It means the fivefold leaders actually doing what Jesus set them in His Church to do—to equip and release others to do ministry.

Surprisingly, these bigger regional expressions don't require a large amount of administration, and are a much better stewardship of our resources than the lost amounts of money in the present real estate debacle of modern churches.

FACILITIES OR FREEDOM?

I am not exactly sure why a small group of believers growing in a home setting suddenly gets dissatisfied with the weekly "building up" of the saints and suddenly decides they need to put the saints in a "building." But I can tell you by firsthand experience, when you get a facility, everything radically changes.

The church was designed to be a movement. That dynamic seems to change rapidly when the church gets an address. Somehow, someway, our infatuation with facilities takes us out of the fluid mode to the maintenance mode in a nano second.

How can we *be* the Church if we keep *going* to church? God wants to have full custody of us rather than just weekend visits. Probably one of the biggest strongholds that keeps us from the freedom offered in the third day is our "edifice complex," and how the building dictates our priorities, our purpose, and consistently aborts our freed passions—all of this, along with simply being a very poor use of our resources.

I have many friends who tell me how they have learned to steward real estate in such a way that it does not dictate to them as to what they do as a church. Trying to use facilities for a sending center, an equipping base, marketplace ministries, etc., is very different than the poorly used facilities of our day that constantly demand upkeep and care.

We rent and use facilities all over our city for the larger regional meetings and conferences we have. We will rent a hotel banquet room, a school auditorium, or even a convention center and invite the fivefold ministers that influence our region to come together to equip the saints.

By networking with the simple house churches and marketplace ministries within our region, we blend together the multi-gifted worship expressions within, and throw one or two of these larger conference-type parties per year, with some of these gatherings actually growing into an *elep*, the word for thousands in Exodus 18:21.

But we do not have to own or become mortgaged to the hilt to successfully use these facilities. The first-century Church grew quite well within the context of organic citywide Church without building buildings to meet in.

Too often, the vision, the flexibility, and the freedom of a local body of believers meeting when God leads and where God leads must submit to the meetings that must happen weekly in the same spot, at the same time, and for the same purpose—mainly to pass the plate to pay the mortgage and steward the budget.

Frost and Hircsch in their book, *The Shaping of Things To Come*, advise church planters to watch for the problem of buildings. It seems most churches that don't have their own sanctuary building are devoted to getting one, but we're not so sure this is always necessary. Church planter Andrew Jopnes cleverly says, "Any church that cannot get by without buildings, finances and paid experts is not fully being church."

Frost and Hirsch go on to state that once a building has been erected, the church program and budget are largely determined by it. In order to service the mortgage, the church has to keep the pews filled and the offerings up. Subtly the building starts to direct the theology presented in it.[2]

I remember in his classic 1975 book, *The Problem of Wineskins*, Howard Snyder writes that church buildings attest to five facts about the Western church: its immobility, inflexibility, lack of fellowship, pride, and class divisions. "The gospel says 'Go,' but our buildings say, 'Stay.' The gospel says, 'Seek the lost,' but our buildings say, 'Let the lost seek the church.'[3]

Only time will tell whether or not we will be able to become fully missional in an institutional age, and so much of that rides on how we use facilities or buildings.

The two phone calls the average pastor makes each Monday upon which his or her identity hangs must stop. The call to the usher for the head count and the call to the treasurer for the coin count get very old, especially when these quantifiers of "nickels" and "noses" are far from the call to "equip and release others."

Paul Viera's new book, *Jesus Has Left the Building*, summarizes the litany of what facilities do and what facilities dictate:

- It's somewhere you go.
- It happens on a special day of the week.
- You have a professional to tell you what to do.
- It requires only attendance and fees paid.
- There exists a hierarchical command structure.
- Meetings come before people.
- It has committees.

- It has programs.
- It has a corporate vision.
- It has a corporate name.
- It segregates itself from other believers.
- It is more concerned with structure than content.
- Quality is sacrificed for quantity.[4]

This house-to-house simple church model tied together with medium-sized worship gatherings and larger regional celebrations and/or conferences really does release to us the best of both the bigger and smaller than church-as-we-know-it paradigm.

Most of us live in a culture that has buildings we can rent and use, many of which sit idle and available during those times when we need them for those larger meetings, those equipping times, those regional expressions.

Meanwhile, our weekly house churches (it is estimated that 20 million adults in America now attend a weekly house church) meet where we live, in what we already have—our homes and apartments, while the schools, clubhouses, recreation centers, auditoriums, and banquet rooms are just waiting to be scheduled and used. And God forbid that we might actually meet outside the four walls in parks, beaches, streets, and campgrounds.

Imagine your normal local church with 50 to 70 percent of its budget going to maintaining the poorly used campus suddenly being released to a house church model. Those monies now can be used for outreach, missions, and people. A single-cell weekend meeting gets multiplied to ten, twenty, thirty simple house churches, with the staff of the church leading through these new house church leaders.

You call these groups together in a rented space for a monthly worship celebration and an annual conference, while the weekly activities are centered around the relational house churches with the ongoing mentoring and coaching of those house church leaders.

Imagine doing this with half the cost of the weekend meeting, and also with the full benefit of the leadership team being able to do their Ephesians 4 job of equipping others.

Barna states in his newest book, *Revolution*, cultural trends indicate an unleashed massive shift in emphasis from the congregational, Sunday, building-based modality to other modalities or expressions of the church. There are other micro-models, like house church, or "simple church" fellowships. These are small aggregations of people who meet in someone's home on a regular basis to fulfill all the functions of a traditional congregation, especially such elements as worship, teaching, fellowship, and stewardship. Barna notes that these groups are not the same as the widespread small groups, cell groups, and home fellowships that are spawned by local churches to supplement what occurs on the local church campus.

There is the *family faith experience* as he describes, which becomes the primary spiritual unit that pursues faith matters, together with parents and their children. *Cyberchurch* refers to the range of spiritual experiences delivered through the Internet. I would also add to this list the shift to the rebirth *marketplace ministries*, where believers function together with like passion in a certain gift or task-driven ministry that becomes their mainstay of Kingdom involvement.[5]

Without grasping the science of all this, we have found portions of this almost invisible network within our geographic sphere, region, and county. They were already living in organic communities through small group relationships and yet were also longing to be a part of a larger worship expression.

The need to practice regional church has become more and more defined. Our goal is to create a permissive atmosphere in which we cultivate the local passions and giftings of people in our larger area, and then to create an umbrella or "covering" that allows these individual ministries, churches, fellowships, and groups to function both within their individual sphere and calling. To do this means to make room and bless all that the Father is doing in the region, and then invite all of these unique expressions to come together for the bigger picture as well.

Our goals have not been just to bless existing ministries, but to help identify, recruit, birth, and engage a whole new generation of believers to see how God wants to use them, all of them. So whether you lead an outreach ministry, or intercession ministry, or care ministry, or ministry to the poor, or an equipping ministry, you are part of the bigger picture of the fabric of the region—His Church in your area, in your locale.

SIMPLE CHURCH

It is a church planter's dream to be encouraging and releasing and planting organic, relational, simple churches, all over the world as a growing missional network.

By 'simple church', we mean a way of doing and being church that is so simple that any believer would respond by saying, "I could do that!"

By 'simple church', we mean the kind of church that is described in the New Testament. Not constrained by structure but by the needs of the extended family, and a desire to extend the Kingdom of God.

By 'simple church', we mean a church that listens to God, follows His leading and obeys His commands.

By 'simple church', we mean spiritual parents raising spiritual sons and daughters to establish their own families.

And by "simple," we do not mean a lower quality of church life. Just the opposite! While no structure or format can guarantee quality, smaller, participatory, family-like environments are ideally suited for today's culture and will assist greatly in helping people to become passionate disciples of Jesus Christ.

But all of this requires a new kind of training for a new kind of church. Years of sitting in traditional church has not prepared us to do church in the manner described in the New Testament. We have been taught to come, to sit, to watch, and to listen to what others have prepared. (Someone described it as "sit, soak and sour.") This is "spectator church," and is no way to train believers to be priests.

By contrast, the Church described in the Bible invites us to engage in a kind of *participatory church*, where everybody talks, laughs, eats, worships, in an atmosphere where all learn, all minister, and all grow.

Simple church, what a thought? No props, no pulpits, no pews, no platforms, no professionals, no public address systems. Simple church, just participation.[6]

We have watched, over the years, as a permissional and missional church gets released in a region. Suddenly, equipping-leaders are equipping, teaching-leaders are teaching, and everyone gets something to do. The dancers dance, the singers sing, the prophets prophesy, the teachers teach, the caregivers care, the vision-casters cast.

The morale of God's people perks up with more hands-on ministry getting done than any planned program could hope to foster. We know that the only way to reach the nations is through the "saints movement," so it is time for Church: simple and regional.

CONCLUSION #2

Regional church is, in fact, a series or network of simple house churches that can gather within a region for worship or equipping.

ENDNOTES

1. C. Peter Wagner, *Apostles and Prophets* (Ventura, CA: Regal, 2000) 39-40.

2. Michael Frost and Alan Hirsch, *The Shaping of Things to Come* (Peabody, MA: Hendrickson Publishers, 2003), 68.

3. Howard Snyder, *Radical Renewal: The Problem of Wineskins Today* (Downers Houston, TX: Touch Publications, 1996), 66-69.

4. Paul Viera, *Jesus Has Left the Building*, http://www.harvest-stone.com.

5. George Barna, *Revolution* (Carol Stream, IL: Tyndale House Publishers, 2005), 64-65.

6. Tony and Felicity Dale, *Simple Church*, http://www.house2house.net.

Chapter Seventeen

THIRD-DAY EPILOGUE

DIETRICH Bonhoeffer wrote in *Life Together*, "God hates visionary dreaming: it makes the dreamer proud and pretentious. The man who fashions a visionary ideal of community demands that it be realized by God, by others and himself. He enters the community of Christians with his demands, sets up his own law, and judges the brethren and God Himself accordingly. He stands adamant, a living reproach to all others in the circle of the brethren. He acts as if he were the creator of the Christian community, as if his dream binds men together. When things don't go his way, he calls the effort a failure. When his ideal picture is destroyed, he sees the community going to smash. So he becomes, first an accuser of his brethren, then an accuser of God, and finally the despairing accuser of himself."[1]

I honestly don't want to become that. I don't want to become one of those presumptuous, narcissistic, proud accusers of the brethren who don't "see" what I "see" and don't "do" things my way. I even wonder about the sheer arrogance and audacity of someone saying that they have a vision for "something new," and then to be so self-aggrandizing that they would actually write about it. As consumers, we are regularly deluged with the magic marketing words of the "new and improved" on the labels of everything we purchase. To propagate something "new," particularly in God's Church, assumes that that which has gone on before is being perceived as having grown old or become outdated, and therefore, also ineffective, dead, or even bad.

STAYING "FRESH"

If we are really saying that permission has been granted to "do" church differently in the third millennium, and we must "do" it now, what does "new" really mean? The last thing we want to recommend is some "new" model that is indiscriminately unleashed on today's church, only to become the disdained model of the next generation.

"New," in order to be "new," and in order to stay "new," must constantly be being made "new," like the technology of our day, whether a computer, a sound system, an entertainment center, or a PDA. The moment you purchase it and walk out of the store, it is becoming outdated, a dinosaur, old stuff. The exponential learning curve for the modern-day inventions of advanced engineering is off the chart. Like built-in extinction, your TV, your DVD player, or your new computer operating system has been designed into a preplanned obsolescence. It's already old. Get used to it.

The Scriptures remind us in Matthew 9, Mark 2, and Luke 5, about this issue of "new" wineskins—this need for "new" containers. But when Jesus uses the analogy of old wineskins and new wine, He actually uses two different words for "new." Some translations say "new" twice. "New" wine must be put into "new" wineskins. The NAS translates it: "new" wine must be put in "fresh" wineskins.

This "new" thing is really more like God's "continually new thing." In Garry Wills' book, *Certain Trumpets*, he notes that Pope John knew that the church must always be in the process of renewal (*ecclesia semper reformanda*) to get back to its original inspiration. Ironically, Wills suggests that this is crucial for the passing along of anything worth giving to another generation.[2]

G.K. Chesterton puts it this way. "Conservatism is based upon the idea that if you leave things alone you leave them as they are. But you do not. If you leave a thing alone you leave it to a torrent of changes. If you leave a white post alone it will soon be a black post. If you particularly want it to be white you must always be painting it again. Briefly, if you want the old white post you must have a new white post."[3]

Some sadly think that because they have or think that they are actually "old" wineskins, they really can't handle any of this "new" stuff. That isn't what Jesus was saying. He is saying, like He did in Revelation 21:5, *"Behold, I make all things new"*—that if you have an old wineskin, get it "represtinated," or restored to its original condition. I have often said how thankful I am that He did not say I make all "new" things.

Staying "new" is not the issue; staying "fresh" to what He is doing is. I am more and more convinced that anything He invades can be "represtinated." God is the "Manna Man." His stuff is *"new every morning"* (Lam. 3:23). And because your future is hidden in your daily routine, this process of change will happen everlastingly daily.

GOD OF THE THEN AND NOW

John Wimber once said that a movement is intrinsically effective for about 20 years. Others have thought that it might be good for maybe a generation. But even that stirs debate as to how long a generation lasts. Is it 30 years? Is it 75 years?

Let's be thankful that the God of the "now" is the God of the generations. He is the God of the past, and He is the God of the "new." He is the Alpha and the Omega. He is the Initiator and the Guarantor. He is the ancient and the modern. He is the forever "Represtinator."

If in reading this book, somewhere along the way you have been inspired to stir up your dreams of new ways, new forms, even new methods of "doing" church, if it has stirred up new passion, then I will be forever thankful. If, on the other hand, you have become angered or dismayed at my arrogance, if you have become offended at my theories, my dogma, my sacrilege to dare to touch your sacred things, and my audacity to demand that a "new," or at least my view of "new," is required, then please forgive me.

I do know that I have found much dissatisfaction and much discouragement among the church leaders who I come across in my travels. In fact, I encounter more frustration and dissatisfaction than it is possible to articulate. Yet, there is no way that simply being different for differences' sake will become the panacea to fix all of that. Adopting some new iconoclastic spirit of entrepreneurship will not become the new magic tonic for all our ills, suddenly making us a perfect church.

I remember one of my colleagues at Bible college who used to remind me that there were only two things wrong with the church—people and Sunday morning!

ABIDE OR PERFORM?

Any true and lasting change that will occur in my life will happen because of Him. It all comes back to the battle of abiding verses performing. Jesus always preferred "abiding" to "doing." He is really into this abiding stuff. That is what He says His vine business has done with you and me, His branches.

This "abiding thing" is more important than the outcome of what we "do." In fact, if we abide, the outcome will always be different than what happens when we just "do" or just perform. It is hard to break that pressure of the Puritan work ethic that so many of us were raised with. All of that Yankee ingenuity is too often rewarded with a certain kind of success and the kudos that follow. The more nickels and noses you can count, the more bucks, budgets, and buildings you can raise, the easier it becomes to be detoured from the freeway of intimacy and abiding, and take you down the off-ramp to the works orientation frontage road of "doing" those bigger and better things for God.

So even with this whole idea of "doing" church differently in the third millennium, we need to be very careful. A great temptation is to think that by just "doing" things differently, there will be lasting change in His Church. It is not only the good news, but the best news, that any true change in how people do "church" will come by and through the Architect of this "ekklesia." There is only One who died for the Church, and this same One who spoke of abiding also said He would take full responsibility for the building of this organism.

Remember what He said: "I will build My church" (Matt. 16:18). Sometimes it is so easy to forget that this whole thing is His, especially with all our titles, business cards, brochures, and websites that have our names, biographical sketches, pedigrees, and pictures plastered all over them.

CONSIDERING OUR DESTINIES

One of those serendipity icebreakers we have used in small groups is to have people write down what their tombstone will say. This is to help us get to know the other person through the revelation of how they see themselves, at least in the arena of how they might be remembered after they have passed. I want to be cautious that mine doesn't read, "He was a real forerunner, a change-agent, a third-day guy, someone who really made things happen." As driven as I am, as type-A as I am, I'd rather be remembered as a lover rather than a doer. I'd rather have God say of me, "Here lays Gary's shell, his earthly container. He really had a heart after Me."

Yes, change is afoot. This is a "new" day. This is a "new" millennium. It is time for a "new" Church. Things will never be the same—that is, except Him. It is He, Jesus Christ, who is the same, yesterday, today, and forever (see Heb. 13:8). So whatever it is that you "do" in your creative and experimental way of leading the segment of His Church that He has entrusted to you, do one thing, and do it best. Rely on Him. Trust Him. Abide in Him, and don't worry about the rest.

Remember...on the third day, anything can happen!

ENDNOTES

1. Dietrich Bonhoffer: *Life Together* (New York, NY: Harper and Row Publishers, 1954), 27-28.

2. Garry Wills, *Certain Trumpets* (New York, NY: Simon & Shuster, 1994), 143.

3. G.K. Chesterton, *Orthodoxy* (New York, NY: Image Books, 1959), 115.

BIBLIOGRAPHY

Allen, Roland. *Missionary Methods, St. Paul's or Ours?* Grand Rapids, MI: Eerdmans, 1962.

Barna, George. *Revolution.* Carol Stream, IL: Tyndale House Publishers, 2005.

Bartleman, Frank. *Azusa Street.* New Kensington, PA: Whitaker House, 1982.

Bickle, Mike. *The Relevant Church.* Orlando, FL: Relevant Books, 2005.

Bonhoffer, Dietrich. *Life Together.* New York, NY: Harper and Row Publishers, 1954.

Chesterton, G.K., *Orthodoxy.* New York, NY: Image Books, 1959.

Cooke, Graham. *A Divine Confrontation.* Shippensburg, PA: Destiny Image Publishing, 1999.

Dale, Tony and Felicity. *Simple Church.* http://www.house2 house.net

Edwards, Gene. *Beyond Radical.* Sargent, GA: The Seedsowers, 1999.

Frost, Michael and Hirsch, Alan, *The Shaping of Things to Come.* Peabody, MA: Hendrickson Publishers, 2003.

Gregory, John Milton. *The Seven Laws of Learning.* Grand Rapids, MI: Baker Book House, 1986.

Gruder, Darrell L. *Missional Community: A Vision for the Sending of the Church in North America*, Grand Rapids, MI: Eerdmans, 1998.

Jackson, Bill. *What in the World Is Happening to Us?*, 1995. http://www.evanwiggs.com/revival/manifest/holylaff.html.

Miller, Calvin. *The Table of Inwardness*. Downers Grove, IL: Inter-Varsity Press, 1984.

Nee, Watchman. *The Normal Christian Church Life*. Anaheim, CA: Living Stream Ministry, 1980.

Simson, Wolgang. *Houses That Change the World*. Waynesboro, GA: Authentic, 2001.

Snyder, Howard, *Radical Renewal: The Problem of Wineskins Today*. Houston, TX: Touch Publications, 1996.

Sweet, Leonard. *EPIC* http://www.next-wave.org/may00/sweet.htm

Theroux, Paul. "Hawaii" *National Geographic Magazine*, December 2002.

Viera, Paul. *Jesus Has Left the Building*. http://www.harvest-stone.com.

Wagner, C. Peter. *Apostles and Prophets*. Ventura, CA: Regal, 2000.

Webber, Robert. *Worship Is a Verb*. Peabody, MA: Hendrickson Publishers, 1992.

White, John. *Simple Church*. www.housechurchchronicles.type-pad.com/

Willimon, W.H. *The Service of God: How Worship and Ethics Are Related*. Nashville, TN: Abingdon, 1983.

Wills, Garry. *Certain Trumpets*. New York, NY: Simon & Shuster, 1994.

About the Authors

GRAHAM COOKE

Graham Cooke is a speaker and author who lives in Vacaville, California where he is part of the leadership team at The Mission, formerly known as Vacaville Christian Life Centre. Graham has been involved in ministry since 1974 and is a popular conference speaker.

He also acts as a consultant to churches going through a period of transition to the next level of their corporate call. He is responsible for a series of training events involving intimacy, warfare, leadership development, and the internationally acclaimed School of Prophecy.

Graham has written two books, *A Divine Confrontation...Birth Pangs of the New Church* and *Developing Your Prophetic Gifting*, and eight interactive journals, *Beholding and Becoming, Towards a Powerful Inner Life, The Language of Promise, The Nature of God, Hiddenness and Manifestation, Crafted Prayer, God's Keeping Power,* and *Living in Dependency and Wonder.*

FUTURE TRAINING INSTITUTE

6391 Leisure Town Road
Vacaville, CA USA 95687
www.grahamcooke.com

GARY GOODELL

Gary Goodell has been doing this ministry stuff for almost 40 years (Foursquare, Vineyard, Third Day). A father of two married children and grandfather of six, his son Brian, wife Cynthia, and their five children (Victoria, Keaton, Maxwell, Savannah, and Jackson), live in Foster City, California, where Brian leads a fellowship in San Mateo called "The Bridge."

His daughter Becky, husband Enrique, with their daughter (Sofia), live in Lake Forest, California. Becky and Enrique are both Psychiatric Technicians at Fairview Hospital in nearby Costa Mesa, and Enrique is enrolled at Vanguard University.

Gary directs *Permission*, a mentoring system for Simple Church, and helps lead *Third Day Churches*. He and his wife Jane, live in San Diego, California.

THIRD DAY CHURCHES

P.O. Box 7531
San Diego, CA USA 92167
www.thirddaychurches.com

PERMISSIONS

Additional copies of this book and other book titles from DESTINY IMAGE are available at your local bookstore.

Call toll free: 1-800-722-6774.

Send a request for a catalog to:

Destiny Image® Publishers, Inc.
P.O. Box 310
Shippensburg, PA 17257-0310

"Speaking to the Purposes of God for this Generation and for the Generations to Come."

For a complete list of our titles, visit us at www.destinyimage.com